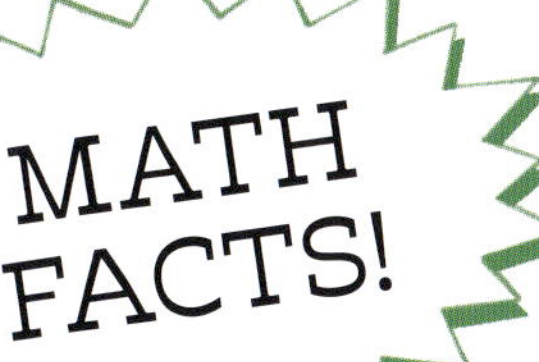

How to Count to

INFINITY

And Other Incredible Ideas About Math

William Potter

Richard Watson

ARCTURUS

This edition published in 2026 by Arcturus Publishing Limited
26/27 Bickels Yard, 151–153 Bermondsey Street,
London SE1 3HA

Author: William Potter
Illustrator: Richard Watson
Consultant: Anna Claybourne
Designer: Sarah Fountain
Editor: Lydia Halliday
Managing Designer: Georgina Wood
Editorial Manager: Becca Clunes

ISBN: 978-1-3988-5754-4
CH012368US
Supplier 29, Date 0925, PI 00009061

Printed in China

Contents

Professor Albert Katzenstein's

Mind-blowing Mathematics

Mathematics seems awfully **COMPLICATED**. Is it useful?
VERY!
7.39 ÷ 5 × 23
We need numbers to help us work out **QUANTITIES**, measure **DISTANCES**, and tell the **TIME**.
That sentence was exactly **15 WORDS LONG**, quite short for you!

We use numbers in **CONSTRUCTION**, for counting materials, and working out **SIZES** and **ANGLES**.
Huff, puff! This building has **1,044 STEPS.**
Why didn't you take the **ELEVATOR**?
There's an elevator?!

Numbers help us organize, plan, and share.
If I have 5 cakes, and I give you 1 ...
You'll have 4 cakes left!

Hmmm. I need more cakes ...
Numbers can help you bake cakes, too, with the measurement of each ingredient and baking time!

Mathematics is used to calculate **SPORTS SCORES** and compare **STATISTICS**.
That's 65 games to you, 0 to me.
Can we play snakes and ladders instead?

Artists use **GEOMETRY** to work out **ANGLES** and **PERSPECTIVES**.
Musicians use numbers to work out the **RHYTHM** and **SPEED** of songs.
DING, DING!

Mathematicians calculate the **DIRECTION** and **SPEED** needed for a spaceship to reach its destination.
And how much **FUEL** it will need.
They can also figure out how the planets and stars move through space.

Numbers help us **BUDGET**, too.
I gave you 40 dollars for shopping. How much change do you have?
Just enough for 2 candy bars!

Count On It

(Numbers)

How to Choose a Lucky Number
What's your **LUCKY NUMBER**, Professor?
I don't believe in luck, Scooter.

But, if I had to pick a number, I'd choose **3**.
Why **3**?

Because of Sir Isaac Newton's **3 LAWS OF MOTION**.
F = d(mv)/dt
N
f
mg sinθ
mg cosθ
mg
θ
F = m d²s/dt²
dp/dt = dp1/dt + dp2/dt
How nerdy ...

I suppose **YOU** have a lucky number, Scooter ...
I do! It's **2**.

Why 2?

Because you'd be nowhere without me as your Number 2!

Numbers are symbols that represent an amount.

Whole numbers, such as 1, 2, 3, and 4, are also called **integers**. These can be divided into **fractions** and **decimals**, and even be **negative**.

We use a set of numbers called the **Hindu-Arabic system**. Different ancient civilizations had different symbols for numbers. Here are just a few ...

	1	2	3	4	5	6	7	8	9	10
Ancient Chinese	一	二	三	四	五	六	七	八	九	十
Ancient Egyptian	I	II	III	IIII	II III	III III	III IIII	IIII IIII	III III III	∩
Ancient Greek	α	β	γ	δ	ε	ϛ	ζ	η	θ	ι
Mayan	•	••	•••	••••	—	• —	•• —	••• —	•••• —	— —
Roman	I	II	III	IV	V	VI	VII	VIII	IX	X

Some numbers are regarded as lucky or unlucky in different cultures. In Western countries, 7 is thought lucky while 13 brings bad luck. Some buildings skip a 13th floor. In bicycle races, the bicyclist given the number 13 wears it upside down.

In Chinese culture, 8 is thought lucky because it sounds like the word for wealth, while 4 is unlucky because it sounds like the word for death!

How Nothing Matters
What are you thinking about?
Nothing.

I AM thinking. I'm thinking about nothing, the number ZERO.
Oh.
I'm in SHOCK! You're ALWAYS busy thinking.

If we didn't have the number 0, how would we write the number between 9 and 11?
Um.

The number 306 means 3 hundreds, 0 tens, and 6 ones. Zero is important.
That's good ...

I just came in to say I've done zero jobs you asked me to.
WHAT?!

NOTHING to it!

Zero is important for describing the quantity of nothing.

The concept was understood about 5,000 years ago, but zero was first used as a number about 1,500 years ago in India.

Zero acts as a placeholder. For example, the number 2,045 equals
2 × 1,000
0 × 100
4 × 10
5 × 1

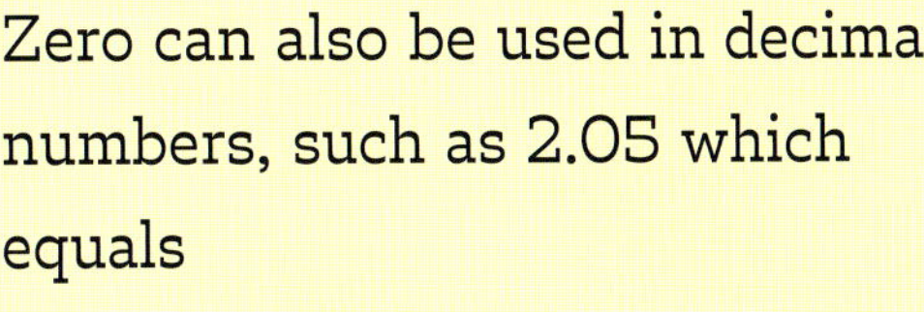

Zero can also be used in decimal numbers, such as 2.05 which equals
2 × 1
0 × tenths
5 × hundredths

Calculations involving 0 produce unique results. Any number + or – 0 is unchanged.

Dividing a number by 0 is not logically possible, but you can divide 0 by a number. This also equals 0!

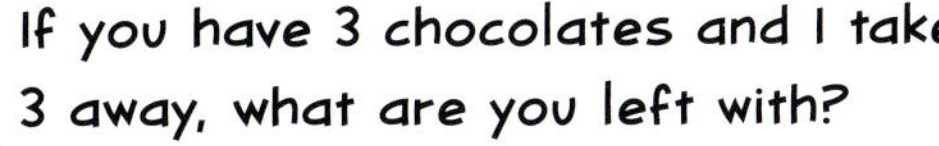

Zero is also essential for computers that use binary (page 26), numbers made up of only 1s and 0s. Without 0, the modern digital world could not function!

How to Pack for a Vacation
I love vacations, but it's so hard to know what to **PACK**!
Just pack the **ESSENTIALS**—books, comfortable leisure wear, and more books.

I don't think I can fit more in!

You're **5 KG OVER** the weight limit. You'll have to remove something.

But there's nothing I don't need.
I'd get bored without my game console ...
... and Teddy just **HAS** to come!

As I said, you just need essentials.
My case is **6 KG UNDER** the limit!

Great! That means Teddy can travel with **YOU**, Professor!

Subtraction is taking away one number from another, like moving backward along a number line.

7 – 4 = 3

You can also think of subtraction as finding the difference between two numbers.

If a weight limit is 20, and Scooter's luggage weighs 25, the difference is 5.

25 – 20 = 5.

10s	1s		10s	1s		10s	1s
6	7	–	4	2	=		

Subtract the 10s first, 6 – 4 = 2.

Then the 1s, 7 – 2 = 5.

So 67 – 42 = 25.

For larger numbers, its helpful to arrange the numbers in columns ...

```
100s 10s 1s
   8   4  7
 – 6   9  2
 ----------

 ----------
```

Start on the right and take away the 1s first, 7 – 2 = 5.

In the 10s column, 4 – 9 doesn't go, so you need to take a 100 from the next column: 8 becomes 7, 4 becomes 14.

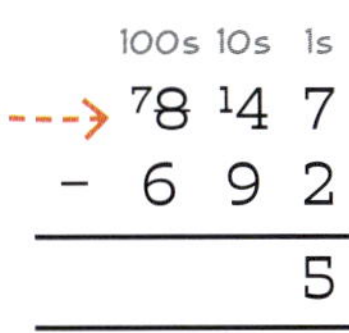

```
100s 10s 1s
  ⁷8  ¹⁴4  7
 – 6   9  2
 ----------
          5
 ----------
```

Now you can continue the calculation

14 – 9 = 5

7 – 6 = 1, and so

```
100s 10s 1s
   8   4  7
 – 6   9  2
 ----------
   1   5  5
 ----------
```

How to Count Like a Centurion
Wow, we're really in Rome!
Yes, we are, and that's the Colosseum.
It'll look amazing when it's finished.

We're here for a mathematics class.
Can't we go on a normal vacation?

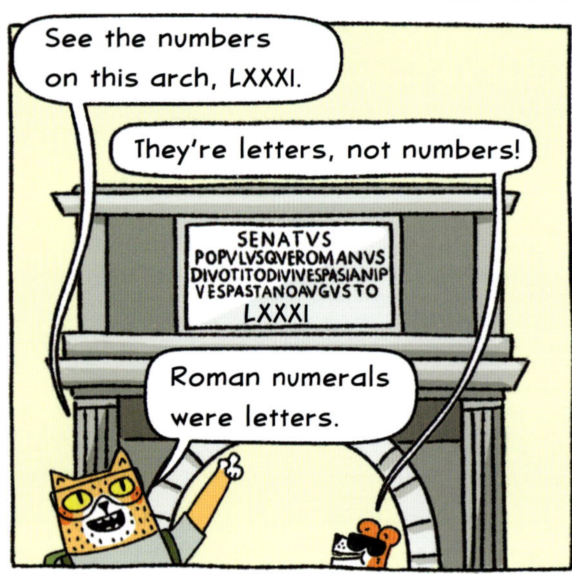
See the numbers on this arch, LXXXI.
They're letters, not numbers!
SENATVS
POPVLVSQVEROMANVS
DIVOTITODIVIVESPASIANIP
VESPASTANOAVGVSTO
LXXXI
Roman numerals were letters.

I II III IV V VI VII
1 2 3 4 5 6 7
VIII IX X L C D M
8 9 10 50 100 500 1000
I represented 1, V was 5, X was 10. I before V or X means one less.

What about **ZERO**?
The Romans didn't have a zero.
And they didn't have a number larger than 1,000, which meant some really long numbers.
2,388 was MMCCCLXXXVIII.

Are Roman numerals still used today?
Yes, you may see them on clocks, chapters in books, and next to the names of kings and queens, like the English King Henry VIII.

Then I am Scooter I!
Scooter I, meet a centurion. Let's ask him about Roman numerals.

I am Maximus Siccius Baculus. I served in the XVI Legion.
That's the 16th Legion, Scooter.

Here's a gladiator.
I won XLII fights to the death!
How many did you lose?

Now we're at the Spanish Steps! Let's count them in Roman ...
I, II, III ...

HUFF PUFF! CXXXIII, CXXXIV, CXXXV ...
Ah! Now this is more my kind of numbers ...

XXXVIII types of ice cream!

How to Be a Billionaire
4, 5, 6, 7 ...
Are those your savings, Scooter?

Yes, if I save a dollar a week, one day I'll be a **BILLIONAIRE**!

I've got 12 dollars so far.
A billionaire, you say ...

Well, at one dollar a week, I calculate it will take you over 19 million years to become a billionaire.
19 MILLION?!

How about a **MILLIONAIRE**?
Just over 19 thousand years.

Forget that, then. I'm going to live like a billionaire today ...
... and spend my 12 dollars on candy!

A **billion** is a thousand million, which means it has 3 more zeros than a million. 1 million: 1,000,000.
1 billion: 1,000,000,000.

For every three zeros added, the number gets a new name. A thousand billion is a trillion, 1,000,000,000,000, followed by a quadrillion, quintillion, sextillion, septillion, octillion, nonillion, decillion ... and so on! One of the best-known big numbers is the **googol**.

There is also a number called a **googolplex**, which is a 1 with googol zeros, but it's too big a number to write down! Even if each digit was the size of an atom, it wouldn't fit in the known Universe!

How to Count to Infinity
What's the biggest number you can think of, Scooter?
5,000,000,000
3,701,987,002
Um ... a googolplex ... PLUS ONE.

Good try, but there are much bigger numbers.
How about a SQUOOGLEPLEX?
You made that up.

I'm thinking about INFINITY.
It's the biggest number there is!
OK, I'll start counting up to it.

You won't be able to. Time would run out before you got there.
What if I started counting up from a million billion?
Same.

Are you sure there's no bigger number?
Yes.

What about infinity ... PLUS ONE?

Infinity is the biggest number. It is written as an endless loop, ∞, like the number 8 on its side.

You can't add 1 to ∞ since it's already the biggest number. It's the same if you multiply infinity by infinity!

$\infty \times \infty = \infty$!

Imagine counting forever.

1, 2, 3 ...

You'd never reach infinity.

The number of ∞ is hard to imagine. It's not an exact number but an idea. Just as counting to infinity is impossible, it would take an **eternity**.

If you had an infinite number of candies and you ate one, you'd still have an infinite number left.

Now I'd like **THAT**!

Some scientists think the Universe is infinite, without ending, and there may even be infinite Universes. There could even be infinite Katzensteins and Scooters!

I think it will take me that long to understand infinity.

How to Be a Prime Suspect
It's **GONE**!
What's gone?
One of my **SPECIAL FORMULAS**.
11 13 17 23

I kept them in numbered jars on the shelf.
2 3 5 7 11 13 17 23 29 31 37 41
43
It looks like a lot of numbers are missing.
I only label them with **PRIME NUMBERS**.

Of course you do ...
Who could have removed it? Who are the **PRIME SUSPECTS**?
Don't look at me! I can't even reach the shelf!

But you could have used **THAT LADDER**!

Wait a minute! Why are there **TWO** number 61s?
2 3 13 17
53 59 61 61 67

Oh.
Number 19 was **UPSIDE DOWN**.
61
19

Prime numbers are whole numbers that can only be divided by themselves or 1 without leaving a remainder.

The first 10 prime numbers are 2, 3, 5, 7, 11, 13, 17, 19, 23, 29.

Think of a number, Scooter.

21.

That's the result of 3 x 7, two prime factors.

What about 12?

That's the result of 2 x 2 x 3!

This is all very interesting, but how can I use prime numbers?

Prime numbers are used in codes for internet security and storing credit card details. This is because there is no pattern to prime numbers so they are impossible to guess. So far, the largest prime number found has over 41 million digits.

All whole numbers (apart from 0 and 1) are either a prime number or the result of multiplying two or more prime numbers called **prime factors.**

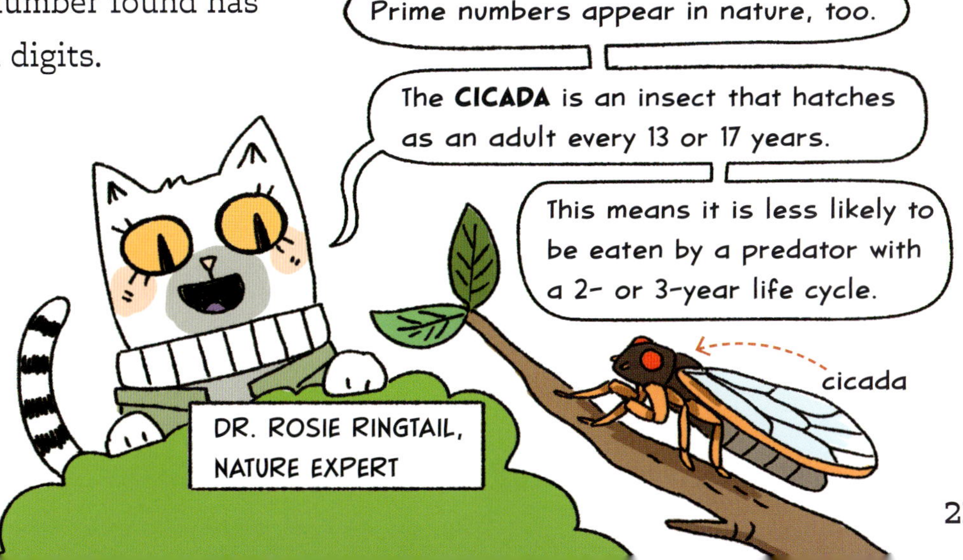

Calculation Station

For large numbers, you can add in columns, adding the 1s on the right first, followed by the 10s, 100s, etc.

$$\begin{array}{r} 3\ 2\ 6 \\ +\,2\ 9\ 3 \\ \hline \\ \hline \end{array} \qquad \begin{array}{r} 3\ 2\ \mathbf{6} \\ +\,2\ 9\ \mathbf{3} \\ \hline \mathbf{9} \\ \hline \end{array} \qquad \begin{array}{r} 3\ \mathbf{2}\ 6 \\ +\,2\ \mathbf{9}\ 3 \\ \hline \mathbf{1}\ 9 \\ \hline {\scriptstyle 1}\ \ \end{array} \qquad \begin{array}{r} \mathbf{3}\ 2\ 6 \\ +\,\mathbf{2}\ 9\ 3 \\ \hline \mathbf{6}\ \mathbf{1}\ \mathbf{9} \\ \hline {\scriptstyle 1}\ \ \end{array}$$

When a column adds up to a two-digit number, you carry the first digit over to add to the next column on the left.

You can also subtract large numbers in columns.

$$\begin{array}{r} 8\ 3\ 7 \\ -\,1\ 5\ 6 \\ \hline \\ \hline \end{array} \qquad \begin{array}{r} 8\ 3\ \mathbf{7} \\ -\,1\ 5\ \mathbf{6} \\ \hline \mathbf{1} \\ \hline \end{array} \qquad \begin{array}{r} \overset{7}{\not{8}}\ {}^{1}\mathbf{3}\ 7 \\ -\,1\ \mathbf{5}\ 6 \\ \hline \mathbf{8}\ 1 \\ \hline \end{array} \qquad \begin{array}{r} \overset{\mathbf{7}}{\not{\mathbf{8}}}\ {}^{1}3\ 7 \\ -\,\mathbf{1}\ 5\ 6 \\ \hline \mathbf{6}\ \mathbf{8}\ \mathbf{1} \\ \hline \end{array}$$

When a bottom row number is larger than the one above, you borrow a number from the digit on its left. In this case, for the 10s, you can do this for 3 – 5. Take 1 from the 8 hundreds to make 13 – 5 = 8.

Multiplication is like adding a number to itself a number of times, so 3 × 5 is the same as 3 + 3 + 3 + 3 + 3. Both equal 15.

Like addition and subtraction, multiplication problems can be answered using columns.

	Step 1	Step 2	Step 3
	2 5 3	2 5 3	2 5 3
×	1 7	1 **7**	**1** 7
		1, 7 7 1	1, 7 7 1
			2, 5 3 0

First you multiply the 7 by 253, then add that to 10 × 253,

7 × 253 = 1,771,
10 × 253 = 2,530

1,771 + 2,530 = 4,301.

Multiplying a number by 10 is easy.

Just add a 0 at the end!

Division is figuring out how many times one number fits into another. You can imagine it like sharing.

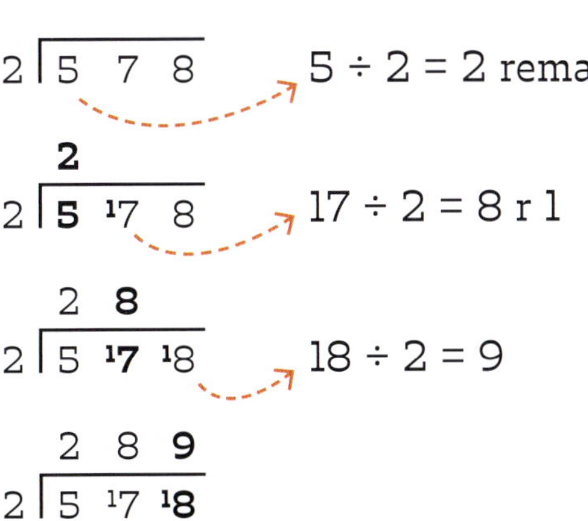

2 ⟌ 5 7 8 → 5 ÷ 2 = 2 remainder 1

2 ⟌ **5** ¹7 8 (quotient **2**) → 17 ÷ 2 = 8 r 1

2 ⟌ 5 **¹7** ¹8 (quotient 2 **8**) → 18 ÷ 2 = 9

2 ⟌ 5 ¹7 **¹8** (quotient 2 8 **9**)

All calculations can be made simpler by tackling them in smaller pieces.

How to Take Shortcuts
What are you looking for, Scooter?
CLATTER!
CLATTER!

A gadget. Didn't you invent a BRAIN BOOSTER to make learning mathematics easier?

There is no such gadget.
You just have to keep studying.
SIGH!

But there are some tricks you can use to make calculations easier!
Yay!

One of the simplest is rounding up or down.
What if I want to add 34 to 29?
Round the 29 up to 30, then later take away 1.

So, 34 + 29 becomes 34 + 30 – 1 = 63!
Thanks. That's my mathematics homework done!

By recognizing patterns, you can use shortcuts to complete some calculations. Rounding up and down is one way.

Times table tricks

4 times table: Double the number, then double it again.

5 times table: Multiply by 10 (add a zero), then halve the answer.

9 times table: You can work out most of the 9 times table using your hands ...

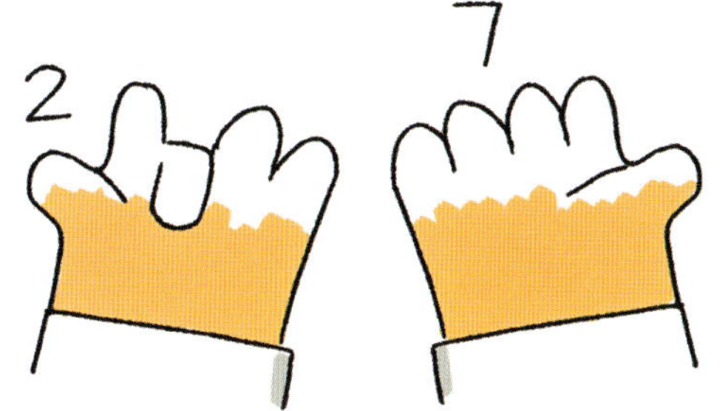

Hold up all ten fingers. If you want to work out 3 x 9, bend your third finger and count those on either side—2 and 7.

3 x 9 = 27.

Division tricks

To figure out if a number is **divisible by 3**, add up all its digits. If they are divisible by 3, so is the number.

For example, 216.

2 + 1 + 6 = 9.

9 is divisible by 3, so is 216.

How to Turn 4 into 100
Is your computer broken?
No, I'm just checking the code.

The computer runs on **BINARY**.
I thought it ran on electricity.

Binary is a **NUMBER SYSTEM**.
We count in 10s using the numbers 0–9, but binary only uses the numbers 0 and 1.

Computers receive instructions as electrical signals, like a switch turning off and on—0 for off, 1 for on—that's binary!

So, your computer doesn't understand the number 4?

No, just zeros and ones. The computer understands 4 as 100.
Wow! I'm **SMARTER** than the computer!

The **binary system**, also known as **base 2**, only uses the digits 0 and 1.

Sorry, won't be needing you today.

Just as the decimal system places 1s, then, 10s, then 100s in columns, the binary system has 1s, 2s, 4s, 8s, and so on. So decimal 2 is 10 in binary, 4 is 100, 8 is 1,000.

Here's how binary numbers build up.

DECIMAL	BINARY
0	0
1	1
2	10
3	11
4	100
5	101
6	110
7	111
8	1000
9	1001

DECIMAL	BINARY
10	1010
11	1011
12	1100
13	1101
14	1110
15	1111
16	10000
17	10001
18	10010
19	10011

1 is the largest number you can have in a column. When you add 1 more, the 1 moves to the next column on the left.

You can also add and subtract in binary just as you would in decimals.

```
8s 4s 2s 1s      8s 4s 2s 1s      8s 4s 2s 1s
    1  1  0          1  1  0          1  1  0
 +  1  0  1       +  1  0  1       +  1  0  1
 ----------       ----------       ----------
          1             1  1       1  0  1  1
 ----------       ----------       ----------
```

In decimal, this calculation would be 6 + 5 = 11.

Computers store information as tiny energy bursts that can be turned on and off like a light switch.

Instructions for this are supplied as 0s and 1s. These numbers are called **bits**. A series of eight 0s and 1s is called a **byte**. A billion bytes is a **gigabyte** (Gb).

In binary, a gigabyte equals 1,073,741,824 bytes rather than 1,000,000,000, due to the way a computer's memory operates.

But you don't need to worry about that.

How to Be Positive

In mathematics, both positive and negative numbers are used. **Positive numbers** are those greater than zero. **Negative numbers** are those less than zero.

This means that if you do a subtraction and the answer is less than zero, you can write in an answer. For example, 15 – 22 = -7.

If you add a negative number to a positive number, you subtract it. 14 + -8 = 6.

If you take away a negative number from a positive number, though, you get a **double negative.**

In the case of 6 – (-4) = , the two negatives cancel each other out, so you get a positive, 6 + 4, so, 6 – (-4) = 10!

Multiplication and division with negative numbers is easy. First, do the calculation ignoring the minus signs on negative numbers, then decide if the answer is positive or negative.

If you subtract a negative number from another negative number, it is the same as adding a positive number. -8 – (-3) = -5.

We put parentheses around the negative number, so it doesn't get confusing with two minus signs together!

The rules are:

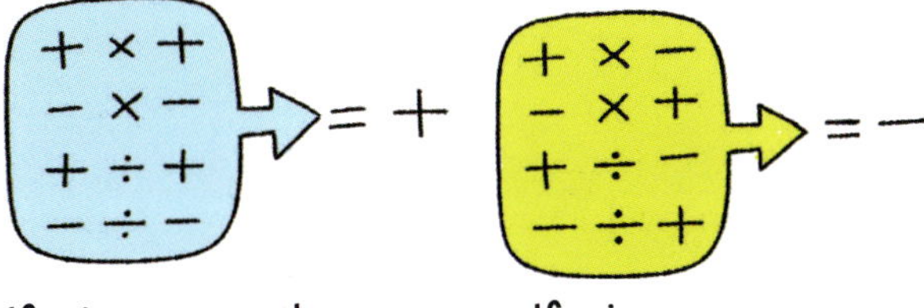

If signs are the **SAME**, the answer is **POSITIVE**.

If signs are **DIFFERENT**, the answer is **NEGATIVE**.

How to Miss a Millennium

Go Figure!

(Squares, Roots, Fractions, and Ratios)

How to
Split a Pizza
I'll divide the pizza!

There are two of us, so I'll cut it in half.

The slices will be too big.
Cut it into four, and we'll have two slices each.

Quarters, then ...

Oh, you're having pizza.
You're welcome to join us, Dr. Ringtail.

So, now I need to cut it into three ...
Thirds will be too big.

Cut each third in half.
I only want one slice.

I knew we should have ordered pasta!

Two slices each for me and the professor, one for Dr. Ringtai ...
Should I cut it into fifths?

Just cut it into sixths.
Why sixths?

I'll have three slices.
That's half the pizza!

That sounds a fraction greedy!

How to Cater for a Party
How is the chocolate cake mix coming along?
Mixing is **EXHAUSTING**!

It'll be worth it.
We have a lot of guests coming to the party!

How many cupcakes do we need?
I'm glad you asked. I've done a **SURVEY**.

We have 20 guests.
$\frac{1}{5}$ are vegan.

$\frac{1}{10}$ are allergic to nuts.
And the ratio of those preferring chocolate to vanilla is 2:3.

The odds of me baking the right selection are a million to one!

A **ratio** is a way of comparing two amounts. Ratios are shown as two numbers with a colon (:) between them.

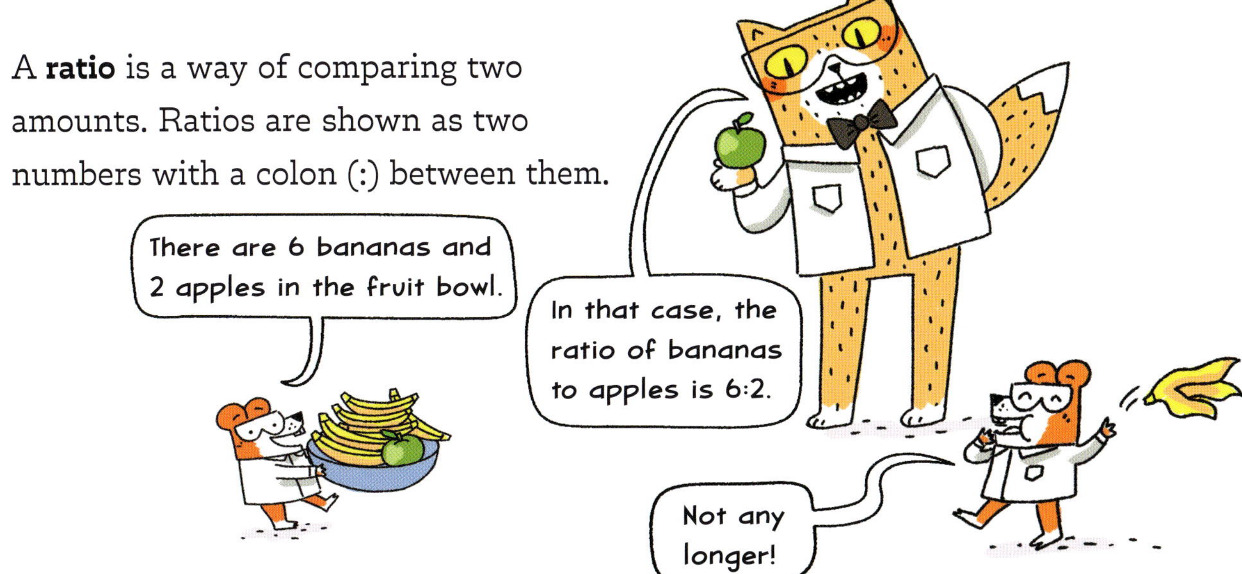

Ratios should be simplified where possible by dividing both numbers in the ratio by the same number.

6 and 2 can be divided by 2, so 6:2 becomes 3:1.
So, there are 3 bananas for every apple.

Ratios are useful in recipes. If the ratio of butter to flour is 2:3, for every 100g (3.5 oz) of butter, you need 150g (5.3 oz) of flour.

A **proportion** measures an amount compared to the total.
If you have 8 lab coats, and 2 of them are size small, the proportion of small coats is $\frac{2}{8}$.
The numbers can be divided by 2 to make the simpler proportion $\frac{1}{4}$.

Proportions can also be shown as percentages.

In this case, the proportion of small lab coats is 25%.

How to Tip
That was delicious!
I'm 110% happy with my dessert!

You can't have more than 100%, Scooter.
Let's pay the check.

We need to add a 20% tip on top.
I only had the kid's menu because I'm little.

OK, so, let's say 30% of this bill is yours ...
... plus a 20% tip.
But you had two desserts...

30 MINUTES LATER ...
Excuse me, gentlemen.

You've taken 50% more time figuring out the check than eating your meal.

A **percentage** (%) is a part of a 100.

Whatever you do, **DON'T** press the red button!

25% is 25 out of 100, 50% is 50 out of 100, and so on.

If your computer has 100 buttons—40 are yellow, 30 are green, 20 are blue, 9 are white, and 1 is red, then 40% are yellow, 30% green, 20% blue, 9% white and just 1% red.

To work out a percentage with other numbers, divide the percentage by 100, then multiply it by the number.

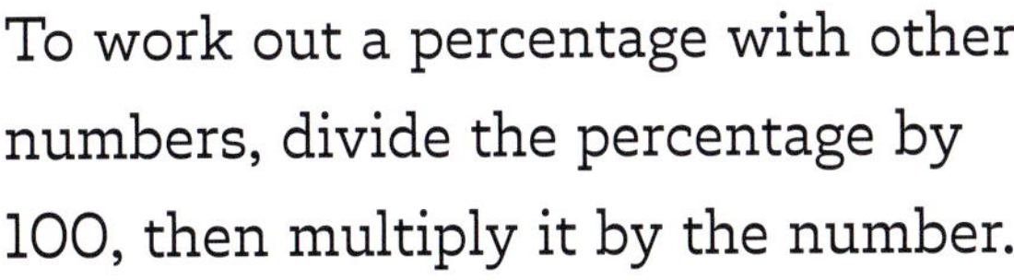

For example, to work out 20% of 25, you need $\frac{20}{100} \times 25$

$\frac{20}{100}$ is the same as $\frac{2}{10}$ or $\frac{1}{5}$

$\frac{1}{5} \times 25 = 5$ so 20% of 25 is 5.

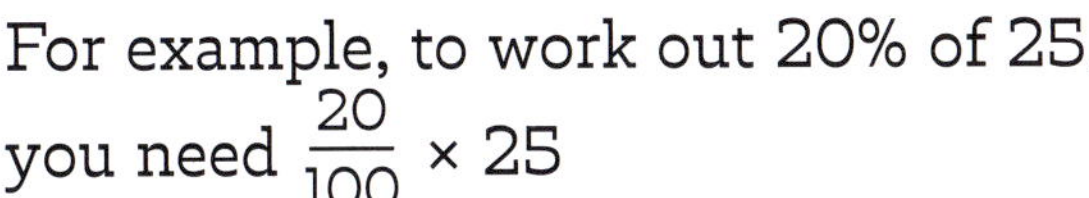

To calculate what percentage a number is, divide the number by the total, and multiply by 100.

If you have 30 balloons and 12 of them are inflated:

$\frac{12}{30} \times 100$

$\frac{12}{30} = \frac{2}{5}$ or 0.4

$0.4 \times 100 = 40$

So 40% of your balloons are inflated.

How to Get the Best Deal
Thanks for helping with the grocery shopping, Professor.
I don't plan to make it a habit.

Shopping makes my brain turn to JELLY.
Ooh, we need to buy some jelly!

Cheesy soup's on special offer. We should buy extra cans!
Not so fast!
20% OFF

We need to check that's it a good deal.
These cans are 20% off but 30% smaller than the other cans.
Sneaky!

And the packs of four only save us a few cents.
What we need to do is calculate the UNIT PRICE for each offer.

I thought you said shopping makes your brain turn to jelly.
I'm not wobbly when it comes to percentages!

Knowing how to work out percentages can save you money.

When you see a special offer in a supermarket with % off or different-sized packages it can be hard to work out if you're getting a good deal or not. What you have to do is work out the **unit price**.

Say you have a choice of

DEAL 1: 200g (7 oz) of chocolate with 50% extra for $4

or

DEAL 2: 100g (3.5 oz) of chocolate, Buy 2 Get 1 Free offer for $3.

Which is the best deal?

Work out the price of 100g (3.5 oz) of chocolate for each deal.

DEAL 1 offers 200g (7 oz) + 50% 100g (3.5 oz) for $4. That's 300g (10.5 oz) for $4, or 100g (3.5 oz) for $1.33.

DEAL 2 offers 300g (10.5 oz) for $3. That's 100g (3.5 oz) for $1.

So, **DEAL 2** is the best.

How to Use Powers

Why are you dressed like a **SUPERHERO**, Scooter?

You said we were going to look at **POWERS**.

Um, I guess I did ...

In mathematics, a power is the number of times a number is multiplied by itself.

3 x 3 = 9, but the answer can also be written as $\mathbf{3^2}$. The small 2 represents the **power of 2**, and means that there are 2 3s in the calculation.

3^2 is called **3 squared**.

It may help to imagine the numbers in squares ...

1	2
3	4

$\mathbf{2^2}$

1	2	3
4	5	6
7	8	9

$\mathbf{3^2}$

1	2	3	4
5	6	7	8
9	10	11	12
13	14	15	16

$\mathbf{4^2}$

2^2 is 2 squares across and 2 down, a total of 4.

3^2 is 3 squares across and 3 down, a total of 9.

4^2 is 4 squares across and 4 down, a total of 16.

Squares from 1 to 10 are:

$1^2 = 1$

$2^2 = 4$

$3^2 = 9$

$4^2 = 16$

$5^2 = 25$

$6^2 = 36$

$7^2 = 49$

$8^2 = 64$

$9^2 = 81$

$10^2 = 100$

Cubes are numbers to the **power of 3**, with a number multiplied by itself not once but twice.

$3 \times 3 \times 3 = 27$, but the answer can also be written as $\mathbf{3^3}$. The small 3 means that there are 3 3s in the calculation.

You can imagine the numbers in cubes ...

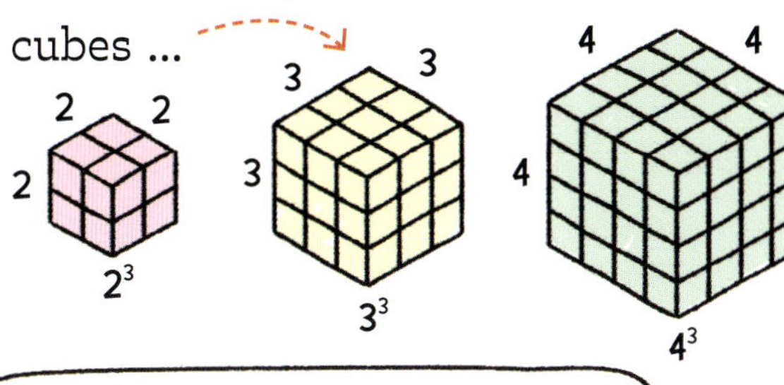

2^3 is $2 \times 2 \times 2$ cubes, a total of 8.
3^3 is $3 \times 3 \times 3$ cubes, a total of 27.
4^3 is $4 \times 4 \times 4$ cubes, a total of 64.

Cubes from 1 to 10 are:

$1^3 = 1$
$2^3 = 8$
$3^3 = 27$
$4^3 = 64$
$5^3 = 125$
$6^3 = 216$
$7^3 = 343$
$8^3 = 512$
$9^3 = 729$
$10^3 = 1{,}000$

Are there even greater powers?

Yes, you can have powers as high as you like!

10^{27}, for example, which is 10 multiplied by itself 27 times, or 1,000, 000,000,000,000,000,000,000,000.

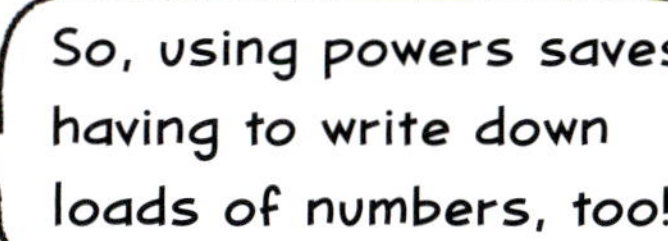

Exactly! So, I can tell you that the Andromeda Galaxy, the nearest galaxy to our Milky Way, is **2.5×10^{22}KM** (2.5 million light-years) away!

How to Measure an Atom
Professor! What are you doing up there?
I'm measuring atoms.
Sorry?

I said, I'm measuring ATOMS.

Atoms are the tiny particles that make up all matter.
Even YOU!

And you need really BIG things to look at really TINY things?
I just like big, complicated machines.

We need REALLY SMALL NUMBERS to describe the size of atoms.
We're talking nanometers, lots of zeroes, and NEGATIVE POWERS!
0.0000000001

You can borrow my smallest ruler, if you like.

Powers can be negative as well as positive.

These powers represent numbers that can be shown as a fraction.

$3^{-1} = \frac{1}{3}$

$10^{-1} = \frac{1}{10}$

$3^{-2} = \frac{1}{3^2}$ or $\frac{1}{9}$

$10^{-2} = \frac{1}{10^2}$ or $\frac{1}{100}$

Just like positive powers, these negative powers are an easier way of writing out a long number.

10^{-9}, for example, is the same as 0.000000001!

Did you just do that calculation in your head?

Some things are so small that they need negative powers to describe them.

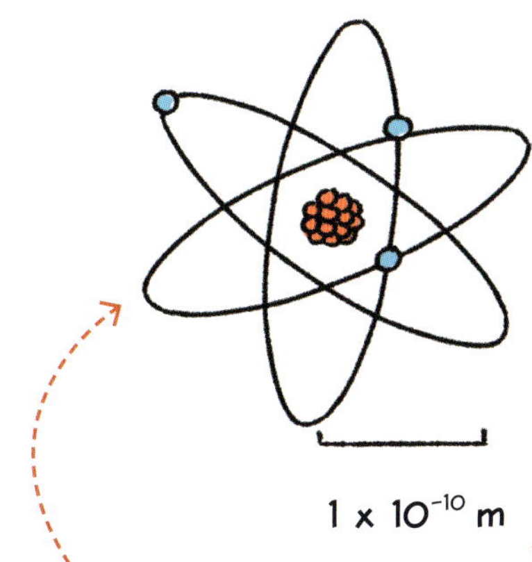

An atom has a radius of 0.1 nanometers or 0.0000000001 meters.

We can write this down as 1×10^{-10} m.

The nucleus of an atom (which contains super-tiny protons and neutrons) is $\frac{1}{10{,}000}$ the size of an atom.

That's 1×10^{-14} m.

How to Discover Your Roots
This is my great-great-great-great-grandfather ARCHIBALD.

And this is my great-great-great-great-great-great aunt JEMIMA.
Why are you showing me these?

You said we were looking at our ROOTS.
I mean SQUARE ROOTS.
?!

You understand that SQUARES are a number multiplied by itself.
Yes.

Well the original number is the square root.
So, 2 is the square root of 4, 3 is the square root of 9.
√9 = √3×3
= 3

So, WHO would be my square root? Archibald or Jemima?

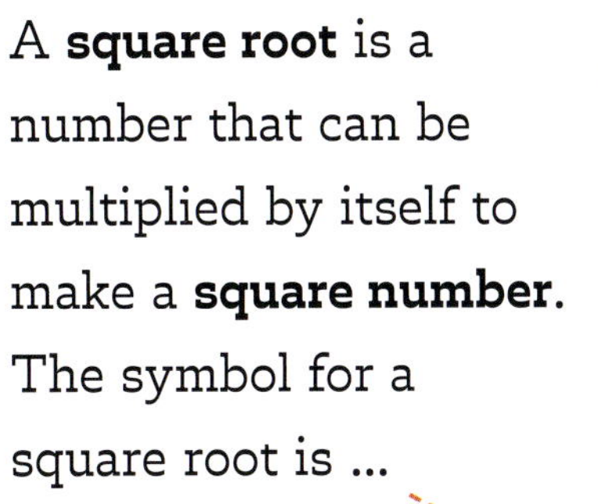

A **square root** is a number that can be multiplied by itself to make a **square number**. The symbol for a square root is ...

For example, $\sqrt{4}$ means "the square root of 4". This symbol is called the **radical**.

$\sqrt{1} = 1$

$\sqrt{4} = 2$

$\sqrt{9} = 3$

$\sqrt{16} = 4$

$\sqrt{25} = 5$

$\sqrt{36} = 6$

$\sqrt{49} = 7$

$\sqrt{64} = 8$

$\sqrt{81} = 9$

$\sqrt{100} = 10$

$\sqrt{121} = 11$

$\sqrt{144} = 12$

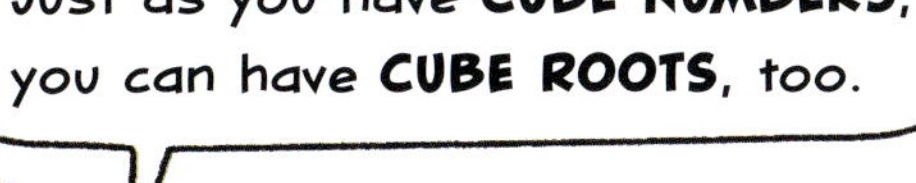

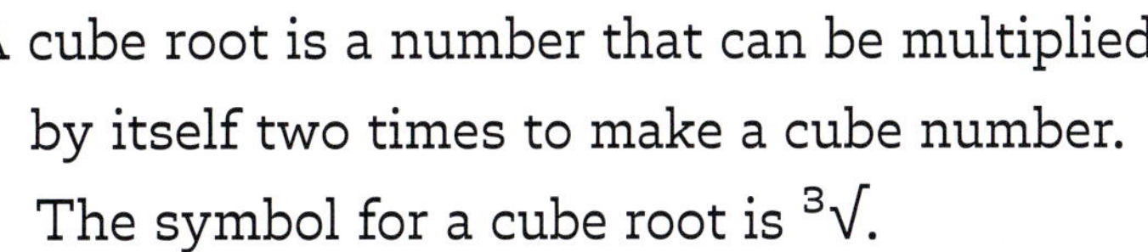

A cube root is a number that can be multiplied by itself two times to make a cube number. The symbol for a cube root is $\sqrt[3]{\ }$.

$2 \times 2 \times 2 = 8$

So, $\sqrt[3]{8}$ is 2!

$3 \times 3 \times 3 = 27$

So, $\sqrt[3]{27}$ is 3!

$\sqrt[3]{8} = 2$

$\sqrt[3]{27} = 3$

$\sqrt[3]{64} = 4$

$\sqrt[3]{125} = 5$

$\sqrt[3]{216} = 6$

$\sqrt[3]{343} = 7$

$\sqrt[3]{512} = 8$

$\sqrt[3]{729} = 9$

$\sqrt[3]{1000} = 10$

How to Go Dotty
Do you need help, Professor?
1.0
4.0
2.0
3.0
9.0
5.0

What are you doing, Scooter?
I'm finishing your dot-to-dot puzzle, joining the numbers ...

It's not a puzzle, I'm just writing down decimal numbers!
The dots are decimal points!

The decimal points separate the whole numbers from numbers less than 1.

How ridiculous that you thought I was preparing a puzzle ...

Oh.

The decimal system can describe not just whole numbers, like 1, 2, 3, 10 or 157, but also smaller fractions or parts of a whole number. The **decimal point** (.) separates a whole number from a smaller part that's between two whole numbers.

Just as each digit left of the decimal point represents **factors of 10**, so do the numbers to the right of the point.

For example, the number 345.76 is 3 hundreds, 4 tens, 5 ones, 7 tenths, and 6 hundredths

Fraction	Decimal
$\frac{3}{4}$	0.75
$\frac{1}{2}$	0.5
$\frac{1}{3}$	0.33
$\frac{1}{4}$	0.25
$\frac{1}{5}$	0.2
$\frac{1}{10}$	0.1
$\frac{1}{100}$	0.01
$\frac{1}{100}$	0.001

You can add, take away, multiply, and divide decimals just as you do whole numbers.

For the calculation 2.4 + 3.7, add each digit as normal, first the tenths then the whole numbers.

0.4 + 0.7 = 1.1

2 + 3 = 5

1.1 + 5 = 6.1, so 2.4 + 3.7 = 6.1

How to Be Irrational
That's a long number ...
It's **PI**.

That's a short word for a long number!

Pi is a value that is equal to the ratio of the circumference of a circle to its diameter.
If you say so.

It's what's called an **IRRATIONAL NUMBER**, with decimal places that go on **FOREVER** with no pattern.

So, how much longer will this print out?
Forever!

Then, should we **REALLY** be printing it out?

For all circles, the **circumference** (distance around the edge of the circle) and **diameter** (distance across a circle through the middle) are in proportion to each other.

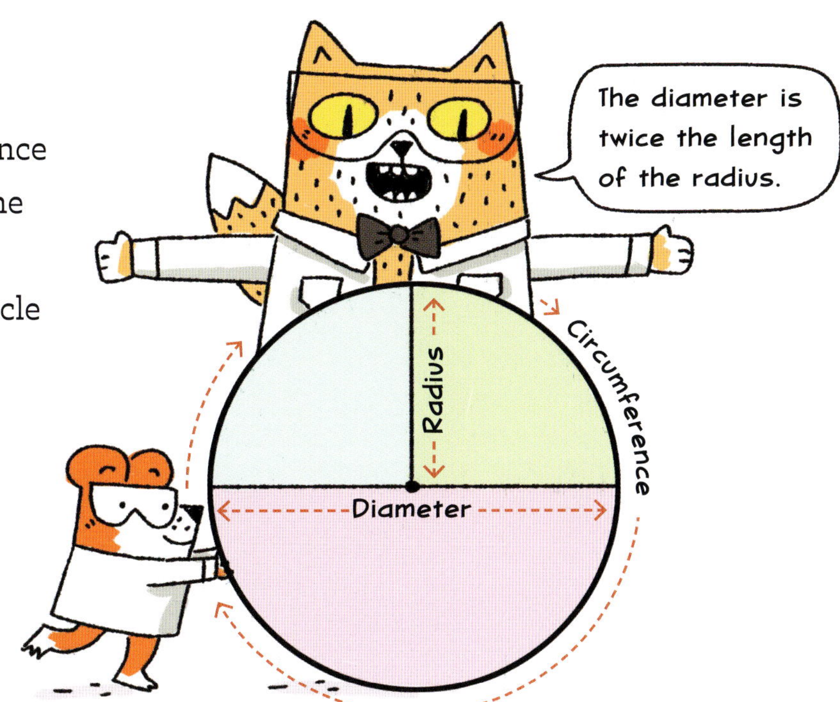

The ratio of the circumference and diameter isn't a simple number though. It involves **pi**. Pi is represented by the Greek letter π.

π = circumference divided by diameter

Circumference = π × diameter

The number known as pi is an endless decimal number! It stars with 3.1415926 ... but goes on forever.

If you want to figure out the circumference of a circle with a diameter of 3 cm:
Circumference = π × 3 cm.

3.14 × 3 cm = 9.42 cm

How to Calculate With Letters

With **algebra** letters, called **unknowns** or **variables**, are used in the place of numbers.

Instead of a calculation with an empty box, you can use a letter.

4 + □ = 10, can become 4 + b = 10.

In this case, b must equal 6.

10 + 3 = c − 6 ...
um ...

You can have several letters in a calculation, such as a + b = c − d.

If you know a = 10, b = 3, and d = 6, you should be able to work out what c equals.

When letters are multiplied, the multiplication sign, ×, is not used, since it can be mistaken for the letter x.

Instead, you just leave the × sign out.

Letters can be multiplied, too, so a × b is written as ab.

Algebra is used in mathematics, graphs, medicine, economics ...

How to Get the Right Formula

A **formula** shows that the relationship between numbers that can vary. It uses letters to represent these values, such as V for volume, H for height, and A for area. When you know some of these values, a formula can help you find others that you don't know.

A = lw, where A is the area, l the length, and w the width. (Remember, "lw" just means "l × w" or length × width).

Another example is a formula used to convert temperatures from Celsius (°C) to Fahrenheit (°F).

$$°F = (°C \times \frac{9}{5}) + 32$$

If the temperature is 20 °C in Celsius, the calculation is

$$F = (20 \times \frac{9}{5}) + 32$$

$$F = 36 + 32$$

$$20\,°C = 68\,°F$$

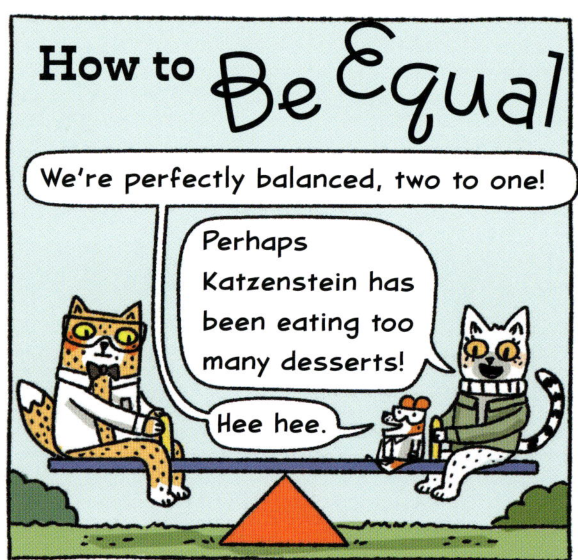
How to Be Equal
We're perfectly balanced, two to one!
Perhaps Katzenstein has been eating too many desserts!
Hee hee.

The middle of a seesaw is like the **EQUAL SIGN** in a calculation.

Both sides of the equal sign should balance.
Are we equals?

Well, that depends what you're measuring ...
Size ... brainpower ... athletic ability ...?

I know you'll beat me with them ...
But you're more than equal to Katzenstein with one value, Scooter ...

Personality!

Get into Shape

(Geometry)

How to Be Right
90 degrees.
90°

That's a **RIGHT ANGLE**.
The right angle for **WHAT**?
90°

It's just a right angle. That's what it's called.
It's a very important angle.

Does that means there's a wrong angle?
Well, every angle that isn't a right angle might be wrong, if you're looking for a right angle.

Are you **ALWAYS** right?

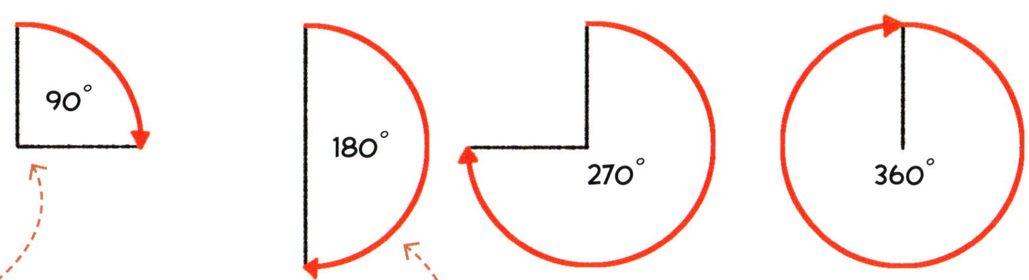

Angles are formed where two lines meet at a shared point. The angle describes the amount of turn between one line and the other. Angles are measured in degrees, using the symbol °.

A right angle is 90°, a quarter turn.

Two right angles makes 180°, a half turn forming a straight line.

270° is three-quarters of a turn.

360° is a full circle.

A right angle is like 15 minutes on a clock!

A right angle has its own symbol, that looks like two sides of a square.

90°

When it appears in a diagram, a right angle is shown as a small square in the corner.

The corners of squares and rectangles are right angles. It's the angle used for doors, windows, and walls.

How to Read a Map
Are you all right, Scooter?
I just thought we might be doing something else today instead of studying COORDINATES ...

Understanding coordinates is important, Scooter.
Imagine you're looking for treasure on a map!

If you say so.
The first coordinate is A3. We have to go north, past the post office.

The next coordinate is F2.
This way ...

Now D5 ...
That takes us to ...

SURPRISE!
Scooter, you didn't really think I'd forgotten it was your BIRTHDAY, did you?

Coordinates are pairs of numbers or letters that show a position on a map or grid. A map is divided into squares. Each square represents a specific area in real life.

With coordinates, the horizontal (side to side) coordinate is always given first, followed by the vertical (up and down) coordinate.

For example, the windmill is in square E2.

If the coordinate is all numbers, such as (2,4), you would count 2 squares across from the left, then 4 squares up from the bottom.

Coordinates are also used on graphs (page 114) with the horizontal line called the **x axis** and the vertical the **y axis**.

As with maps, the horizontal coordinate is listed first, so Scooter is on (3,4).

Graphs may also include negative coordinates. Katzenstein is on (-2,-3).

Are negative coordinates for when you're going backward?

How to
Take a Turn
Are you sure this is safe?
We'll soon find out.
What?!

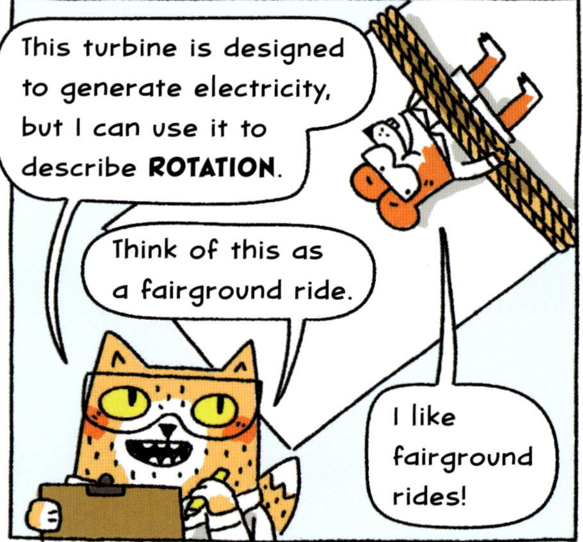
This turbine is designed to generate electricity, but I can use it to describe ROTATION.
Think of this as a fairground ride.
I like fairground rides!

You're turned 90 DEGREES around a CENTER OF ROTATION between the four sails.

Now you are the right way up after turning 180 DEGREES.
It's spinning faster!

Now you've made a COMPLETE TURN.
The wind's picking up ...

Tell me about itttttttttttttttttttt!

Rotation transforms an object or shape by turning it around a fixed point called the **center of rotation.**

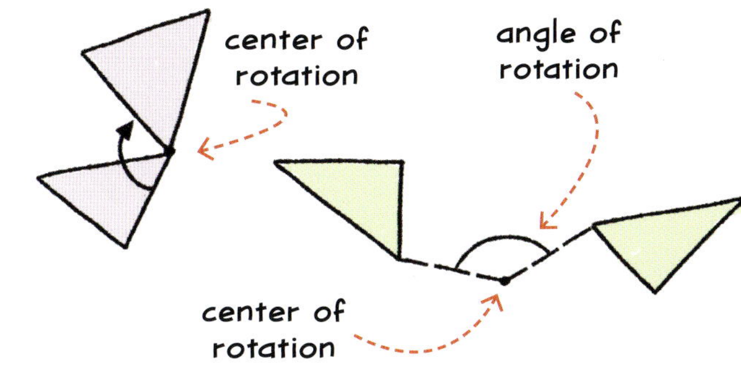

The center of rotation may be the center of a shape, a corner, or even a point away from the shape. The amount that it turns is called the **angle of rotation.** Any point on the shape will remain the same distance from the center of rotation as it turns.

To work out where a shape will end up after a rotation, you need to know the center and angle of rotation.

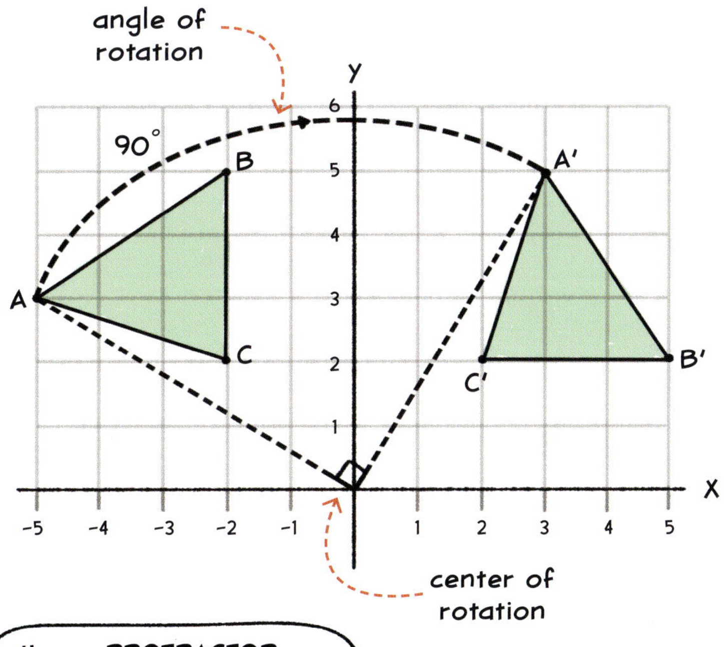

Use a **COMPASS** to draw arcs from each corner of your shape in the direction of rotation.

Use a **PROTRACTOR** to mark the angle of rotation on each arc.

Join the points to draw your shape in its new rotated position!

How to
Match Up
Keep still, Scooter. This is going to be your official photo.
Make sure you get my **BEST SIDE**.

Scooter, you're practically **SYMMETRICAL**!
How rude!

Symmetrical means matching both sides of an axis.

Your left side matches your right side.
I still prefer this side.

Please keep still!
Well, I caught your best side ...
CLICK!

... the back!

A shape has **symmetry** when a line can be drawn through it that divides it exactly in two.

There are two types of symmetry—**reflective** and **rotational.**

Reflective symmetry is when one side of the shape looks like a mirror image of the other.

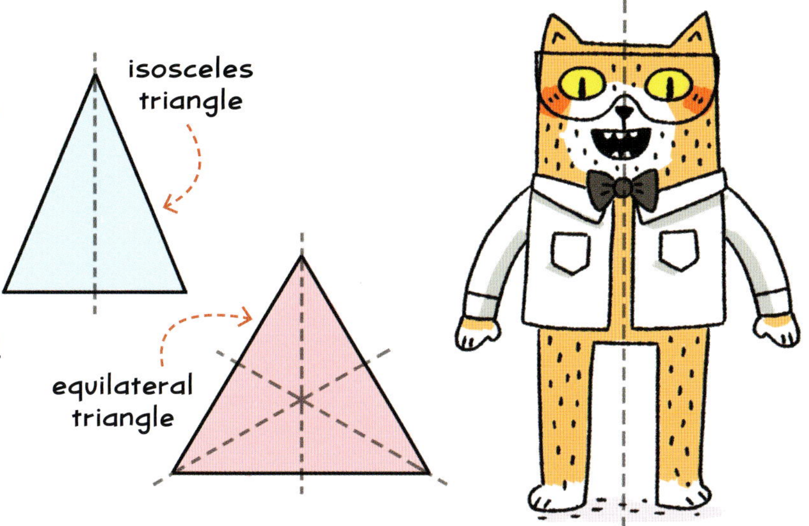

The **isosceles triangle**, above, has one line of symmetry. The **equilateral triangle** has three lines of symmetry. Some shapes have more.

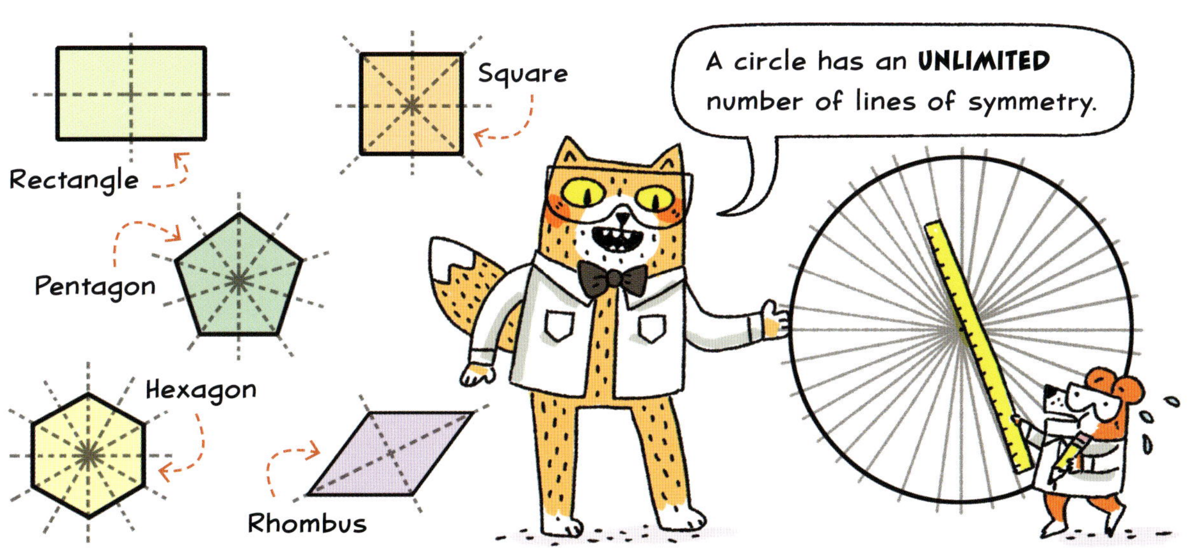

Rotational symmetry works when a shape is rotated around a point called the **center of rotation** to fit its original outline.

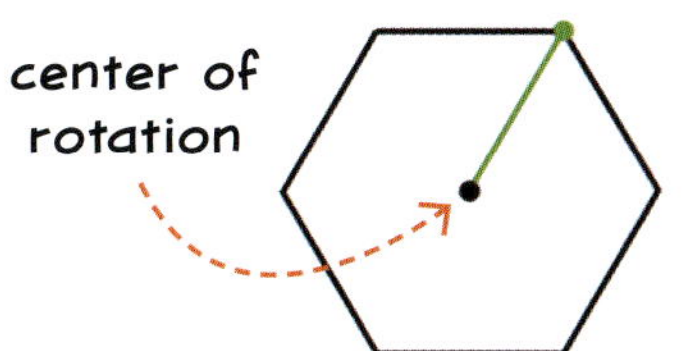

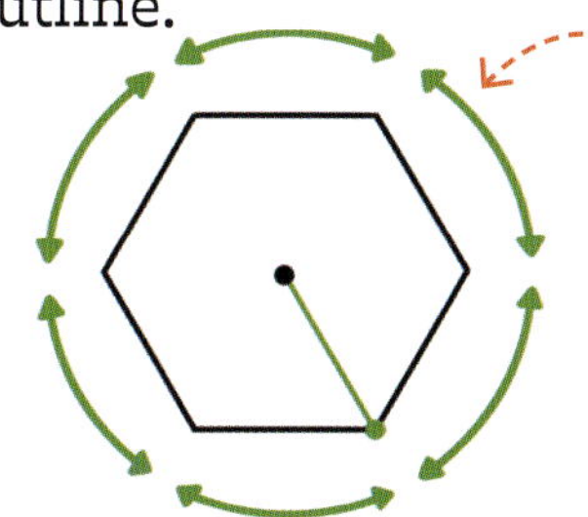

A hexagon, for example, can be rotated around its center and fit its outline 6 times during a complete turn. This means it has an **order of rotational symmetry** of 6.

How to Be the Opposite
Admiring your reflection?

Actually, I'm doing some calculations.
Right ...

A reflection shows the mirror image of an object. Every point on the image is the same distance from the line or axis of reflection as the original.
So?

I can feed this information into my duplicating device to create a MIRROR-KATZENSTEIN!
Have you thought this through ...?

Here he is! What a handsome fellow!
Hello, Mirror-Me!

Goodbye, Katzenstein!
Ah! He's talking backward. I'll need to operate the translator.

Goodbye, Katzenstein!
He says the opposite, goodbye instead of hello!
Well, he is a Mirror-Me!

Mirror-Me, help me input this data into the computer.
No.
He said no, but he's still doing it!

He's inputting all the wrong data! He's doing it all backward!
Mirror-Me, stop!
Mirror-Me go!
Stop, stop!
Mirror-Me, clean the lab instead.
No.

He's making a mess of everything! It's because he's a mirror-image, so he's doing the opposite!
Make more mess, Mirror-Katz!

How to
Build a Model
It's here!
DING DONG!

What's here?
My **ROCKET KIT**!

I was expecting it to be bigger ...

It still seems small.
How can I use it to go into space?

This is a **MODEL** rocket, Scooter, **1:144 SCALE**.
That means it's 144th the size of a real rocket.
Oh.

Can I use it to send a **BUG** into space?

Scaling makes something larger or smaller but keeps everything in exact proportion. It is used for architectural and engineering plans and for creating accurate models. Scooter, on the right, has a scale factor of 1:2 or $\frac{1}{2}$.

Meet mini-me!

The image is half the size of the original.

Scooter

Scooter, 1:2

Scale is written as two numbers or measures divided by a colon (:), which represents the ratio between the figures.

If you see 1 cm: 1 km on a map, this means that every cm on the map represents a km of real distance.

It doesn't look far on the map!

It's miles away, Scooter!

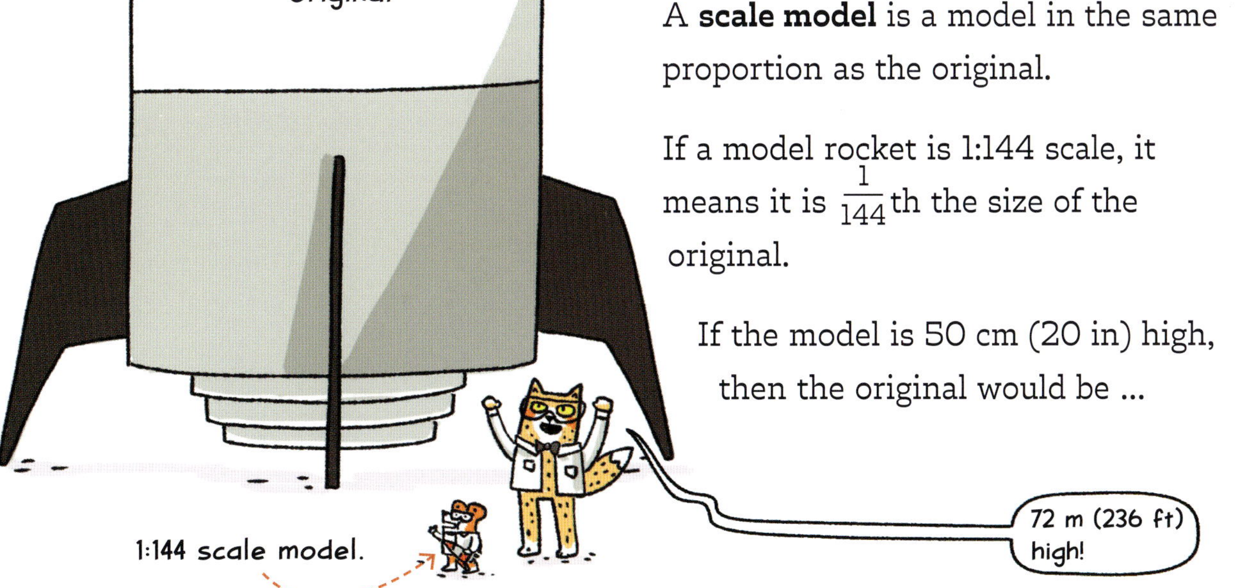

A **scale model** is a model in the same proportion as the original.

If a model rocket is 1:144 scale, it means it is $\frac{1}{144}$th the size of the original.

If the model is 50 cm (20 in) high, then the original would be ...

How to Make the Perfect Sandwich

A triangle is a **polygon**—a flat shape with straight sides. Triangles have three sides.

There are several different types of triangle.

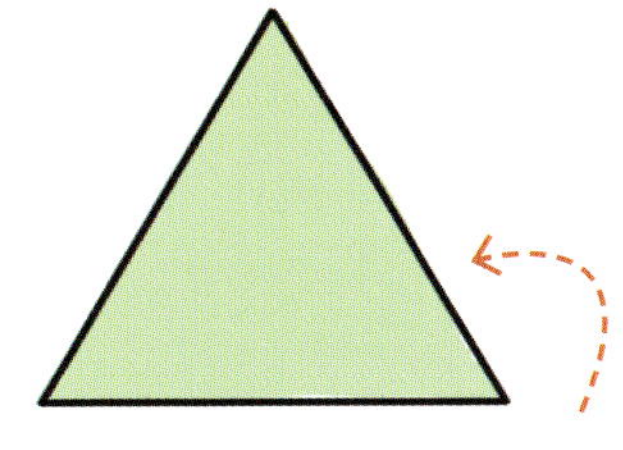

EQUILATERAL TRIANGLE
A triangle with three equal sides and three angles that all measure 60°

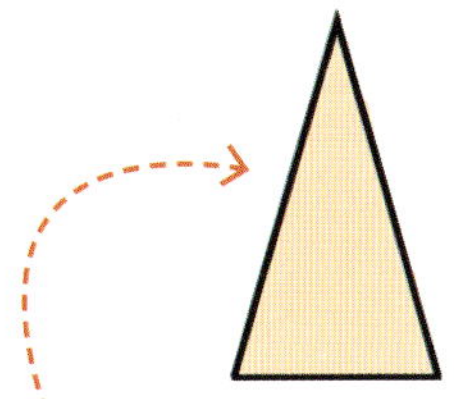

ISOSCELES TRIANGLE
A triangle with two equal sides and two equal angles

SCALENE TRIANGLE
A triangle with sides of different lengths and angles of all different sizes

The longest side of a triangle is opposite the largest angle. The shortest side is opposite the smallest angle.

The internal angles in any triangle add up to 180°.

How to Live Like a Bee
Let's see if my bees are ready to share some honey with us.
Are you sure we won't get stung?

These protective clothes will keep the bees from us.
But a little smoke will keep them calm, too.

Look at the wax honeycomb the bees have made.
It's made up of **HEXAGONS**, shapes with six matching sides!

Hexagons are efficient shapes.
They provide space for storing pollen and honey and form a strong supporting structure.

Now would you like to taste some fresh honey?
Would I?!

Mmmm! Supersweet!
Help! I think I've got a bee in my bonnet!

Hexagons are another type of **polygon**. A hexagon has six sides and six angles.

Hexagons are an excellent shape for forming a grid of cells. With six equal sides, they fit together perfectly, with no wasted space, and build a strong frame, like the bees' honeycomb.

Honeycombs aren't the only natural hexagons.

The plates along a turtle's shell are hexagon-shaped!

Bees also have compound eyes many made of many tiny hexagons.

Aargh! Giant bee!

Any polygon can be divided into triangles. Since the angles inside a triangle always add up to 180°, these can be used to work out the angles inside and outside the shape.

Joining opposite corners of a regular hexagon forms six **equilateral triangles**, each with three 60° angles. As two of these triangles fit in each corner of the hexagon, you can work out the angle for each corner of a regular hexagon ...

$2 \times 60° = 120°$.

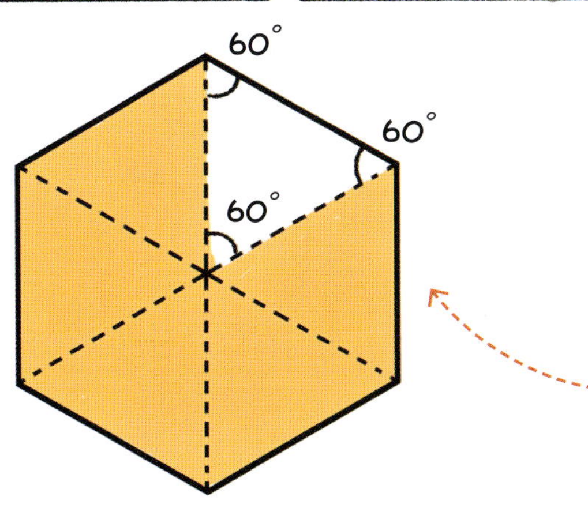

With six angles in a hexagon, the total of the internal angles is:

$6 \times 120° = 720°$.

Measure Triangles With Squares

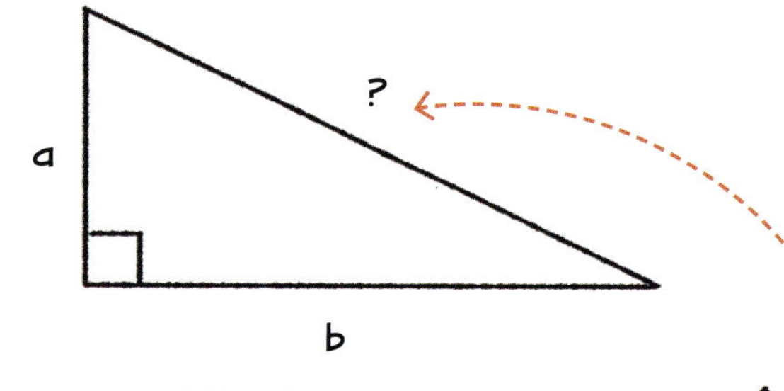

If you know the length of two sides on a right-angled triangle, you can can work out the length of the other one by using **Pythagoras' theorem.**

Pythagoras' theorem says that the sum of the squares of the two short sides on a right-angled triangle equal the square of the longest side.

This is described by the formula $a^2 + b^2 = c^2$.

Pythagoras discovered the relationship between the sides when he placed squares against each length.

He found that the area of the two smaller squares matched that of the large square.

In this example,

$a = 3$, $b = 4$

$3^2 = 9$, $4^2 = 16$

A square along the hypotenuse made up of squares the same size would be $5^2 = 25$.

If $a^2 + b^2 = c^2$,
then $a^2 = c^2 - b^2$.

If $c = 5$, and $b = 4$,
$a^2 = 5^2 - 4^2$.

$5^2 - 4^2 = 25 - 16 = 9$.

The square root of 9 is 3!

So, using Pythagoras' theorem, you can measure triangles with squares!

How Not to Be Square

Squares are four-sided shapes with four sides of equal length and four 90°, or **right angles** (page 56).

They are just one type of **quadrilateral**, or four-sided shape. Here are some other types.

All 4 sides and angles are equal

RECTANGLE
All 4 angles are equal, and opposite sides are equal

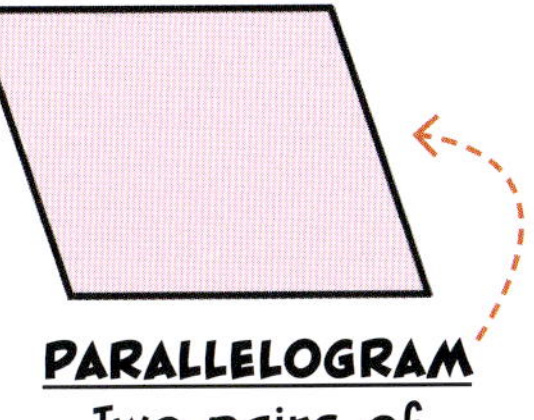

PARALLELOGRAM
Two pairs of parallel sides and two pairs of equal angles

All 4 sides are equal

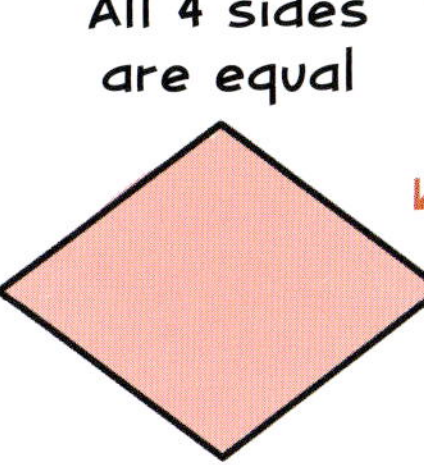

KITE
Two pairs of equal sides and two pairs of matching angles

CONCAVE KITE
Two pairs of adjacent equal sides, one angle greater than 180°

TRAPEZOID
One pair of parallel sides

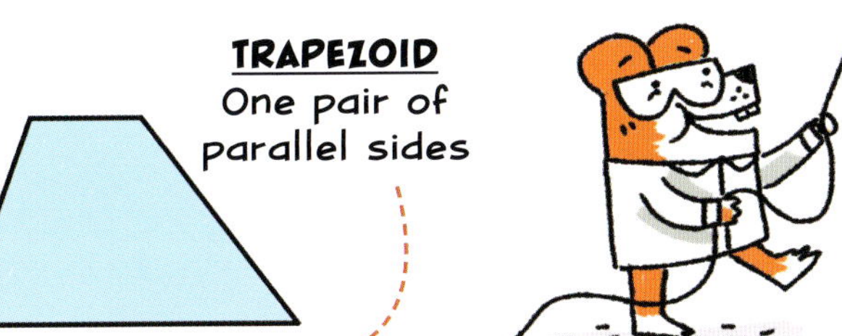

ISOSCELES TRAPEZOID
One pair of parallel sides and two pairs of equal angles

Any quadrilateral can be split into two triangles.

The sum of the angles in a triangle equals 180°, so the sum of the angles in a quadrilateral equals 360°.

How to
Be Endless

Why are you staring at that circle, Scooter?
I'm trying to find its start.

It's a circle, Scooter, one continuous closed curved line surrounding a center point!
Every point on its circumference is the same distance from the center.

You won't find a start!

... and don't bother trying to find its **END** either!
End?

A **circle** is a shape made up of one curving, continuous line that goes around a central point and remains at the same distance from it.

The parts of a circle have names:

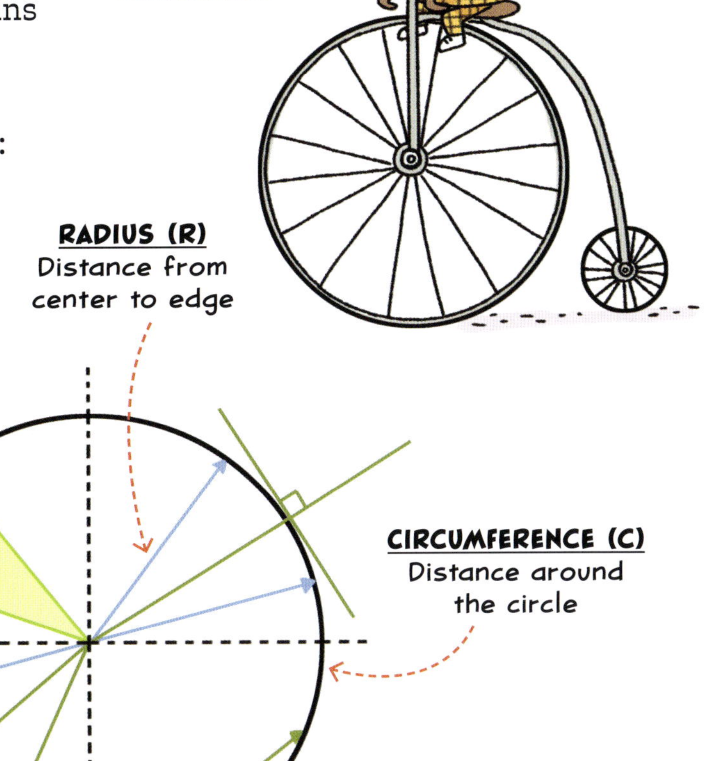

The circumference and diameter of a circle are in proportion to one another and can be calculated using the letter pi (π, page 48).

The circumference of a circle = $\pi \times$ diameter.

The area of a circle = πr^2 (the radius squared, multiplied by π.)

How to Be Solid
Would you like to go into another dimension, Scooter?
Oh, yes, please!

Oh. This is a CUBE.
Yes, while your SQUARE is a 2-DIMENSIONAL shape, a cube is a 3-DIMENSIONAL shape.

Other 3D shapes include, spheres, cylinders, and pyramids.

What's the matter, Scooter?
When you said go into another dimension, I thought we might travel to the future ...

We can do that, too!

Ten minutes later.
Is that IT?!

Measure Up

(Measurements)

Made to Measure

Measurements are used to accurately describe the size of things. There are two main systems used for measuring: **metric** and **imperial.**

	METRIC	IMPERIAL (US CUSTOMARY UNITS)
LENGTH	millimeter (mm), centimeter (cm), meter (m), kilometer (km)	inch (in), foot (ft), yard (yd), mile (mi)
MASS or WEIGHT	milligram (mg), gram (g), kilogram (kg), tonne	ounce (oz), pound (lb), ton
VOLUME	milliliter (ml), centiliter (cl), liter (l)	pint (pt) gallon (gl)

Only three countries don't use the metric system: the United States, Liberia, and Myanmar. The United Kingdom uses both systems.

Length is the distance between two points. We use it to measure how long something is or how far a journey may be.

We can also use lengths to measure **area**.

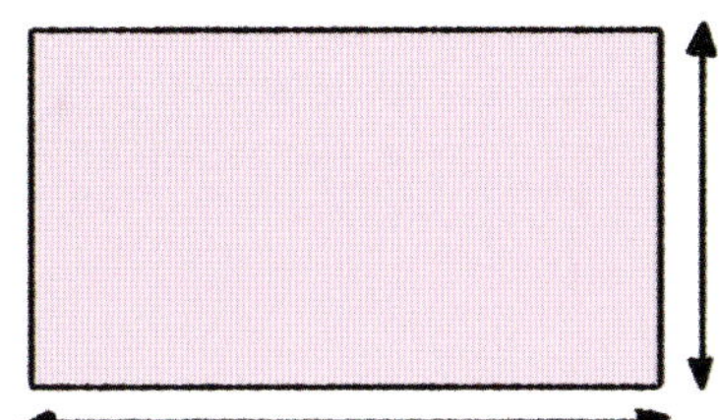

When measuring the **area** of a rectangle, we measure the length and width in the same units. If the lengths are measured in **centimeters** (cm) then the area will be in **square centimeters** (cm^2).

Area = length × width

When measuring the **volume** of a block we measure the length, width, and height.
If the lengths are measured in **centimeters** (cm), then the volume will be in **cubic centimeters** (cm^3).

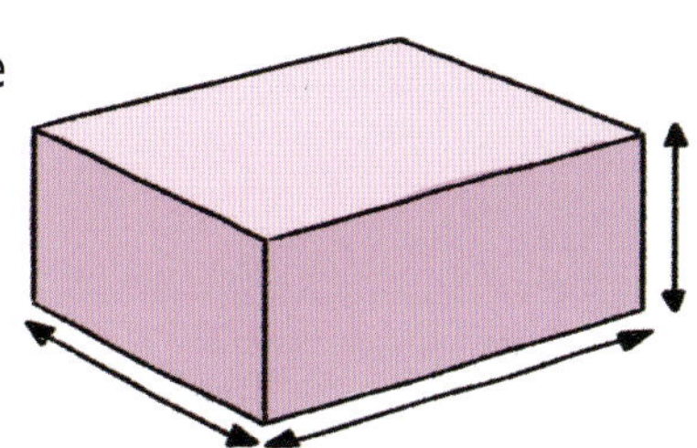

Volume = length × width × height

Time is measured in seconds, minutes, hours, days, weeks, months, and years.

Yay! It's almost lunchtime!

Speed is the distance moved in an amount of time.

Speed = $\frac{\textbf{Distance}}{\textbf{Time}}$

If Katzenstein bicycles 10km (6.2 mi) in 2 hours, he had an average speed of 5km/h (3.1 mph).

How to Measure a Plot
Another wonderful harvest from my veg plot!
Wow!

How big is your plot?
You can measure it for me if you like.

But I don't have my MEASURING TAPE!
I'm sure you'll work something out.

I've measured it!
Oh good. How big is it?

28 square cucumbers!

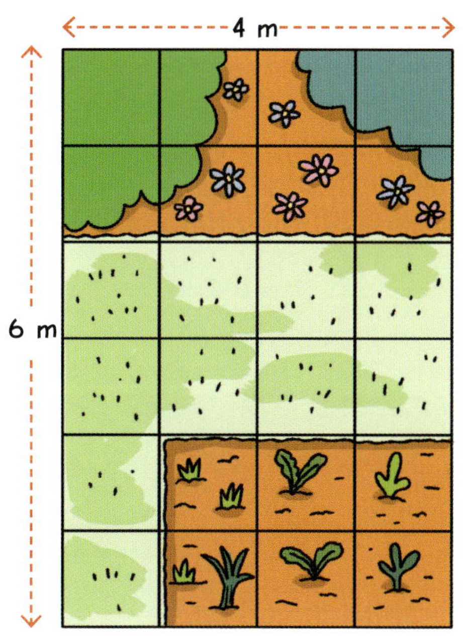

Area = length × width

Area is measured in square units.
If a garden is 6 meters longs and 4 meters wide, it has an area of:
6 m × 4 m = 24 **square meters** (m^2).

You can imagine this as a group of 24 squares, each 1 m × 1 m.

Not all areas are squares or rectangles, but they can still be measured.

If the squares in this grid are all 1 m^2, what is the area of the red shape?

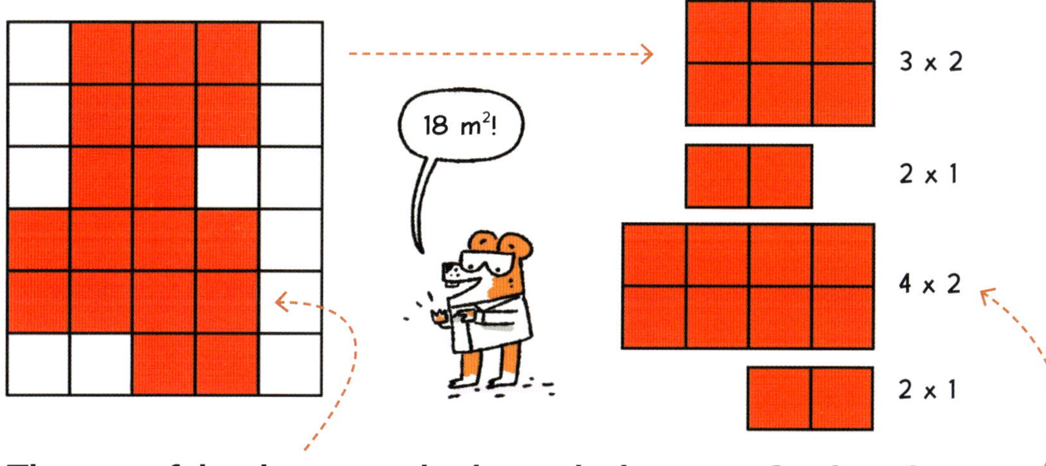

The area of the shape can also be worked out by measuring the length and width of each rectangle, then adding them together.

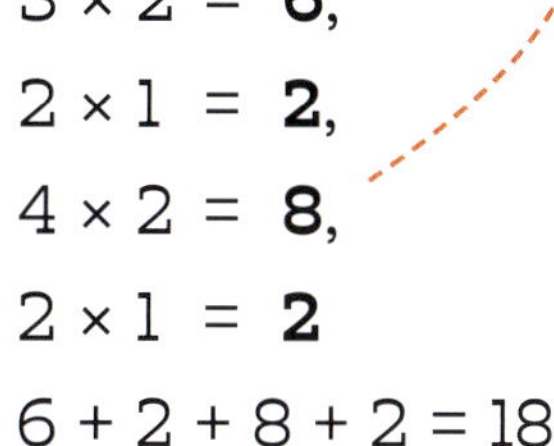

3 × 2 = **6**,
2 × 1 = **2**,
4 × 2 = **8**,
2 × 1 = **2**
6 + 2 + 8 + 2 = 18

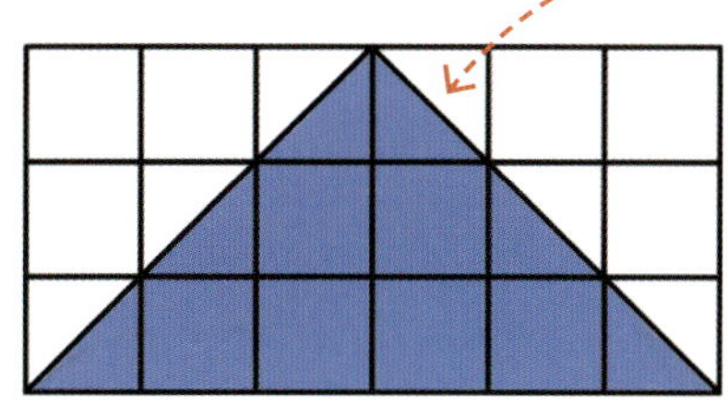

This triangle fills 6 whole squares and 6 half squares. Its area can be worked out, too: 6 + 3 = 9 squares.

How to Invent a Measure
Is a FOOT as long my foot or your foot?
Neither. It's probably as long as the person who invented the foot's foot.

Are they still alive so I can borrow their foot?
Afraid not. The foot was first used over 4,000 years ago!

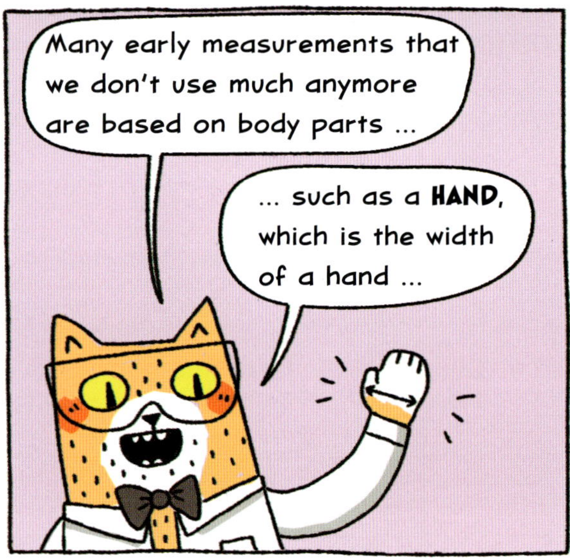
Many early measurements that we don't use much anymore are based on body parts ...
... such as a HAND, which is the width of a hand ...

... and a CUBIT, which was the distance from the elbow to the top of the middle finger ...

... and a butt ...
A BUTT?!

A butt is a measure of volume in barrels equal to two HOGSHEADS.
Now you're just making them up!
Certainly not.

And then there's the **SMOOT**, a length based on the height of a student named Oliver Smoot ...

If you had a measure named after you, what would it measure?
A **KATZENSTEIN** would have to be a measure of **BRAINPOWER**!

What about a **SCOOTER**?
Well, certainly not **HEIGHT** ...

... or speed ...

... or energy.
There's only one thing a Scooter can measure ...

... **SCOOTERNESS**!

How to Go Metric
Ounces, pounds?! I need to convert these measurements from IMPERIAL to METRIC!

Let me help you with these calculations ...
One ounce equals 28 grams.

I need 10 ounces of flour.
That's 280 grams.

Now I need 6 ounces of honey.
So multiply 6 by 28 ...
... so that's 168 grams.

One hour later ...
Are you happy with your cake, Scooter?

I think it tasted better in IMPERIAL.

The imperial measurement system can be hard to remember.

1 pound = 16 ounces

1 gallon = 8 pints

The metric system uses the decimal system, so measurements go up in 10s.

"Kilo" means 1,000, "centi" means $\frac{1}{100}$, and "milli" means $\frac{1}{1{,}000}$.

1 kilometer = 1,000 meters

1 meter = 100 centimeters

Metric:

Length is measured in millimeters (mm), centimeters (cm), meters (m), and kilometers (km).

Weight is measured in grams (g) and kilograms (kg).

Volume is measured in milliliters (ml) and liters (l).

Metric measures go from the very large to the very small. The diameter of our galaxy, the Milky Way, is about 1.2 **zettameters**. A zettameter is one billion billion meters!

An electron in an atom is thought to be about 1 **attometer**, a billionth of a billionth of a meter, or 10^{-18}m.

How to Fill Space

Volume is a measure of how much space something occupies. It is measured in cubic units, such as cubic centimeters (cm^3) or cubic inches.

Some 3D shapes are easy to work out the volumes for, such as cubes and cuboids. You just need to multiply the length, width, and height.

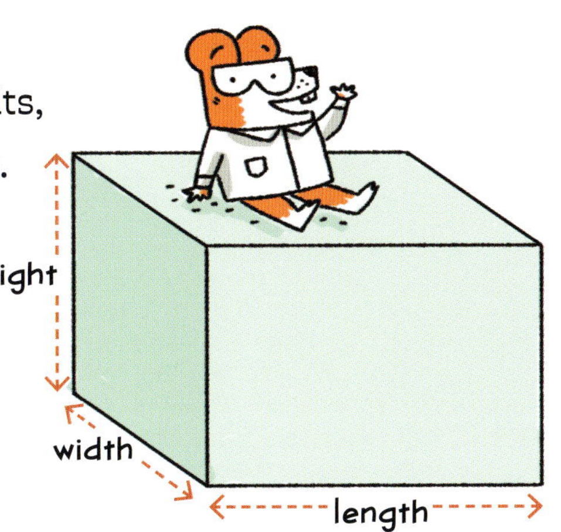

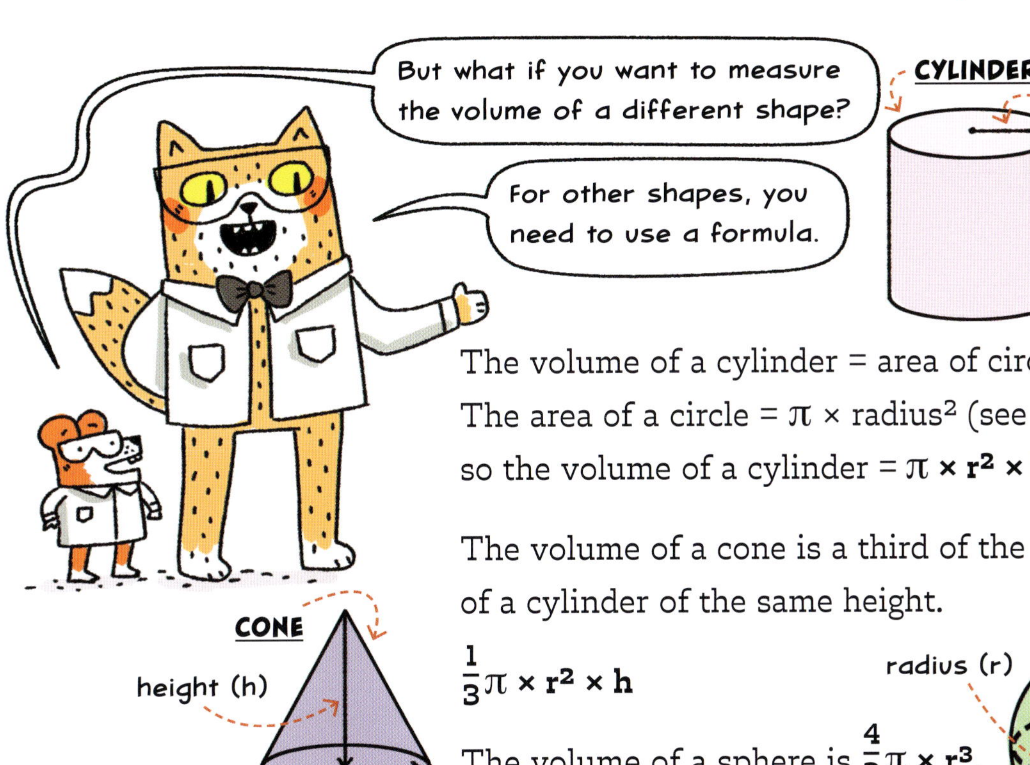

The volume of a cylinder = area of circle × height. The area of a circle = $\pi \times \text{radius}^2$ (see page 48), so the volume of a cylinder = $\pi \times r^2 \times h$.

The volume of a cone is a third of the volume of a cylinder of the same height.

$$\frac{1}{3}\pi \times r^2 \times h$$

The volume of a sphere is $\frac{4}{3}\pi \times r^3$.

Capacity is a measure of how much space is available in a container. It can be measured in milliliters and liters (metric) or pints and gallons (imperial).

If a tank has a capacity of 40 liters, and 30 liters is poured into it, there is 10 liters of capacity left.

How to Measure the Earth
Scooter, could you measure the CIRCUMFERENCE of the Earth?

Circumference?
That's the distance around it.

Not this globe, the REAL Earth!
Oh.

Some time later ...
Well, I'm packed. I have sandwiches and a long tape measure!
I may be gone a while. I'll send you a postcard.

You don't need to leave home, Scooter ...
... oh, he's gone.

Five minutes later ...
That was quick!
I finished all the sandwiches before I reached the bus stop.

Over 2,200 years ago, the Greek mathematician Eratosthenes, knowing the Earth was round, managed to work out how big it was.

He set up a pole in Alexandria, Egypt, and measured the length of its shadow at noon. By drawing a triangle, he was able to work out that the angle of the Sun's rays was 7.2°.

1. Creating a 7.2° shadow on tilted ground.

2. Hitting the rod directly and creating no shadow.

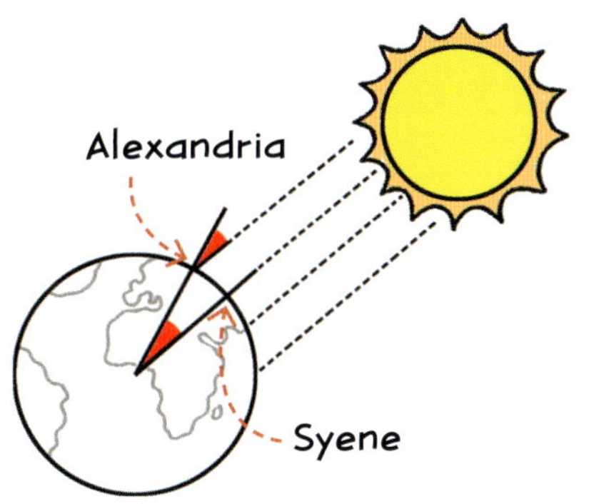

In Alexandria, the Sun cast a 7.2° shadow. In Syene, the Sun was right overhead and cast no shadow.

The Sun is so far away its light hits Earth in straight lines. For it to hit Alexandria at an angle meant that the city was turned away from the Sun.

Eratosthenes knew Syene was 800 km (500 miles) away. Using this information, he was able to work out the **circumference** of the Earth.

If 800 km (500 miles) was 7.2°, then 360°, a full circle, equals 40,000 km (24,850 miles).

How to Measure With a Shadow
Here we are, Scooter!
The **GREAT PYRAMIDS OF GIZA**!

I'm waiting.
What for?
I'm waiting for you to turn this trip into something to do with mathematics.

OK, tell me the height of the tallest pyramid without climbing to the top.

Or looking in the guidebook.

Excuse me, could you tell me how tall is the Great Pyramid?

You can work out the height of an object without holding a tape measure from the bottom to the top.

You can use right-angled triangles (page 56) instead!

That's not the way, Scooter.

Around 2,600 years ago, in ancient Egypt, the Greek mathematician Thales noticed that, at a certain time of the day, his shadow was the same length as his height.

Thales realized this made a **right-angled triangle** and that when this happened, all other objects would have have shadows that were the same length as their height too.

Thales used this method to find the height of the Great Pyramid. Since his shadow matched his height, the pyramid's would too—so he just had to measure its shadow!

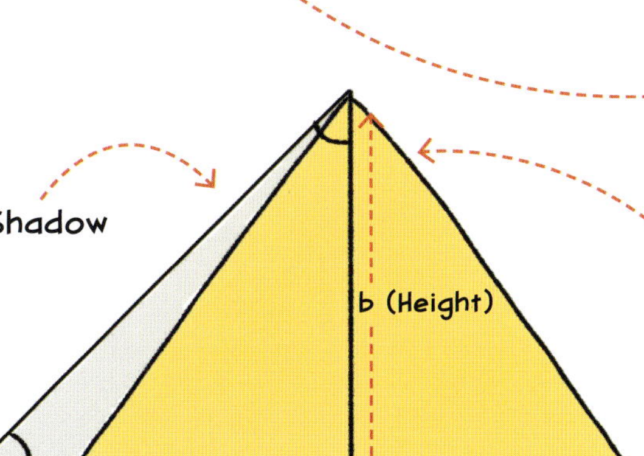

The length from the highest point of the pyramid to the end of the shadow matched its height!

How to Avoid Falling Trees

You can calculate the height of a tree without climbing up it by using **trigonometry**.

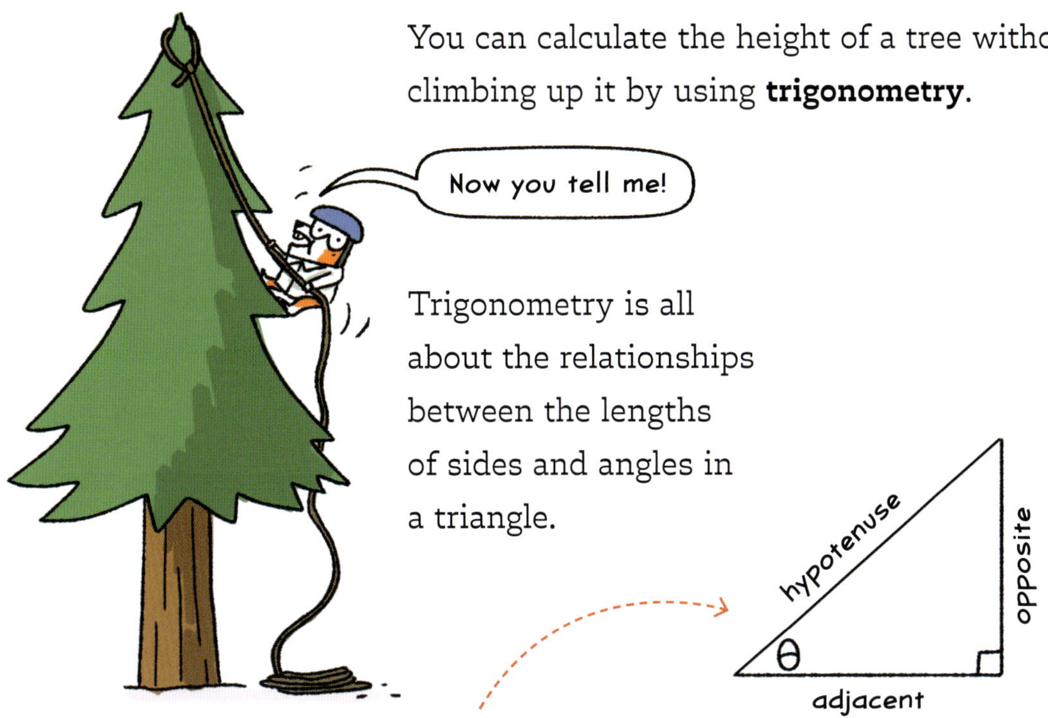

Trigonometry is all about the relationships between the lengths of sides and angles in a triangle.

For a right-angled triangle, the long side is always called the **hypotenuse**. The other sides are called the **adjacent** and the **opposite**. The names of these sides interchange depending on which angle we are using. To find the height of the opposite side here, we need to know two things—the length of the adjacent side and the angle between the hypotenuse and the adjacent side. This angle is marked with the symbol θ.

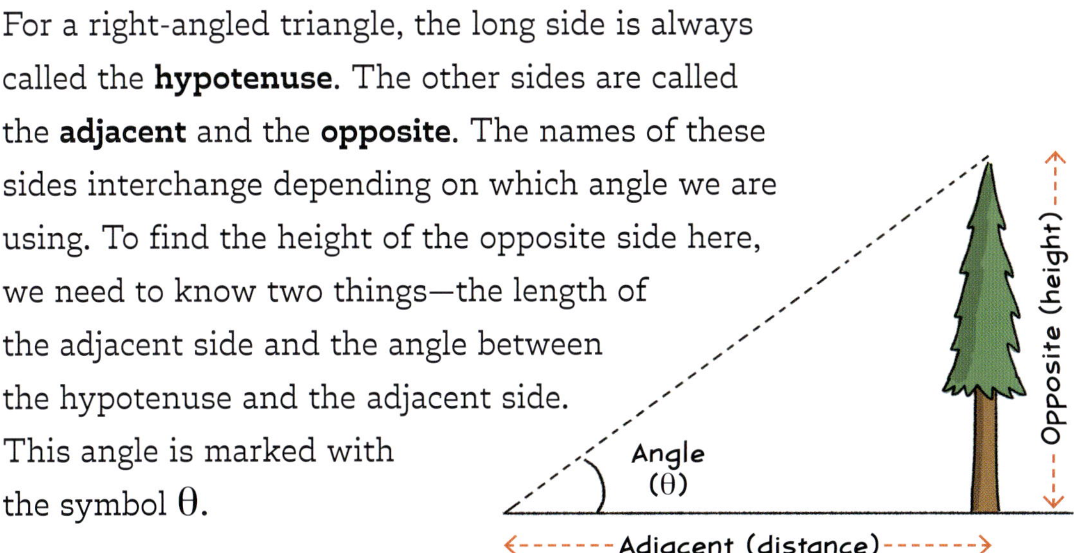

To find out the height of the tree, in this case we need to use a formula called **tan** on a calculator. There are also other formulas, called **cos** and **sin**.

Opposite (height) = tan θ × adjacent (distance)

So if the angle is 35° and the adjacent is 10 m (33 ft), then we can calculate the height of the tree. The value for 35° tan is 0.7, so:
0.7 × 10 m (33 ft) = 7 m (23 ft).

How to Keep Time Like a Babylonian
SIGH! There's never enough time in the day to do all of my jobs.

Professor, why do we only have 60 minutes in an hour?
That's because of the BABYLONIANS. They counted in 60s.

Can we ask them to add more minutes in an hour?
They lived over 5,000 years ago, Scooter.

So we don't need their permission!

If we added more minutes to an hour, we'd have fewer hours in the day.

That's OK. I could do without 2 to 3 in the morning.

Over 5,000 years ago, the Babylonians of West Asia developed a system of mathematics based around the number 60, rather than 10, like the decimal system (page 46).

60 seconds = a minute
60 minutes = an hour

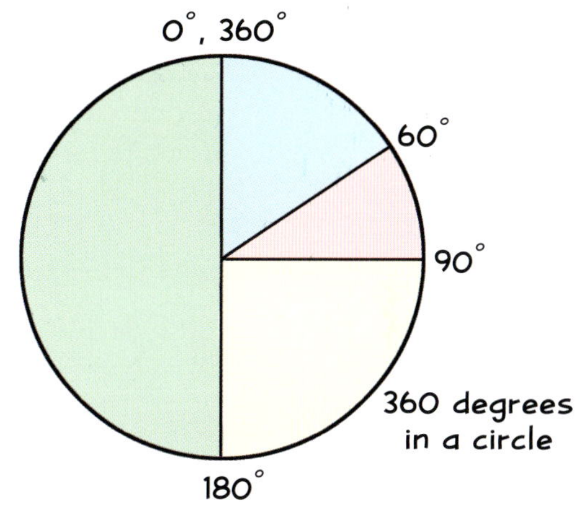

Time is based on the movement of the Earth around the Sun.

A **day** is how long it takes the Earth to make a complete turn on its axis. And this is split into 24 **hours**, 1,440 **minutes**, and 86,400 **seconds**.

A **YEAR** is how long it takes the Earth to complete one orbit of the Sun—365 days, 6 hours, 9 minutes.

If a year's 365 days, what happens to those extra hours and minutes?

Every four years, we have a **LEAP YEAR** with 366 days instead of 365.

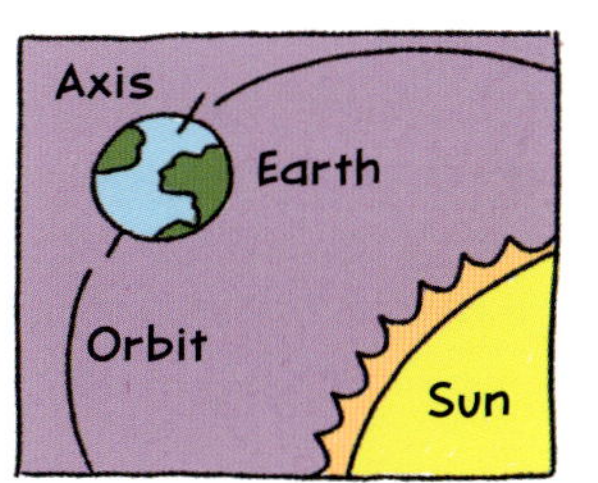

How to Light Up the Dance Floor
Hit those beats, Professor DJ!

1-2-3-4 ...

Why did you count 1-2-3-4?
TUM-
TUM-
TUM-TUM!
That's a count in. Musicians use it as a guide so they know when to start playing and what speed to play.

This music has a speed of 120 beats per minute.
TUM-
TUM-
TUM-
TUM!

This tune is 160 beats per minute.
TE-TE-
TE-
TE-
TE-
TE-
TE-TE-TE-TE!

It's **TOO FAST**!
I can feel my heart racing at 160 beats per minute!

Musicians use different time signatures, too!
This song is in $\frac{4}{4}$ time, which means it has 4 beats for every bar of music.
TAP TAP TAP TAP!

This tune is called a **WALTZ**. It is in $\frac{3}{4}$ time, which means it has 3 beats for every bar of music.
DA-DA-DUM! DA-DA-DUM!

And here are several tunes played in different time signatures and speeds ...
DA-BOK-DUM
PAK - POK - BONK!

DA - POK - DUM
I can't dance to **THIS**!
PAK - POK - BONK!

What time would you like?

Time you stopped being the DJ!

How to
Be Balanced

What are you doing with my supply of cakes and cookies, Professor?
I'm just testing a theory ...

Now, just sit here.

AMAZING!

How do you do it, Scooter?
Do what?

How do you eat your OWN WEIGHT in cakes and cookies every week?!

Weight is how heavy something is due to the force of **gravity** pulling on it.

It is measured in **grams** and **kilograms** (metric) or **pounds** and **ounces** (imperial).

There are 1,000 grams (g) in a kilogram (kg).

There are 16 ounces (oz) in a pound (lb).

Balance scales have a pan on either side of a pivot. To work out the weight of an object, known weights of different sizes are placed in the opposite pan until the scales are perfectly balanced.

Modern scales are electronic. You first check that the readout is zero before placing objects on the scale. Electronic scales can provide readouts in both metric and imperial measures.

How to Keep a Log

In the past, sailors would release a wooden float on a knotted rope called a **LOGLINE** into the water.

They counted the number of knots released as the ship sailed for an amount of time.

Get Organized

(Sequences and Statistics)

How to Get in Order
3 days ago.
Only 6 cookies left.
They're delicious!

2 days ago.
4 cookies.
Half gone.

Yesterday.
The last 2 cookies!
You should have baked more!

4 days ago.
8 freshly baked cookies. Four for you, four for me.
They smell delicious!

6, 4, 2 ... 8?! This is out of SEQUENCE!

I prefer a happy ending.

A sequence is a series of numbers that follow a pattern. If you know the pattern, you can work out the next number in the sequence.

The first number in a sequence is called the 1st term, the second is the 2nd term, and so on ...

3, 5, 7, 9, ...

1st term
2nd term
3rd term

And the dots?

The dots mean the sequence continues.

Some patterns are easy to work out, such as adding three each time.

1, 4, 7, 10, 13, ...

Some are more complicated, with a two-step formula needed to make the next number.

2, 3, 5, 9, 17, ...

The formula is, multiply by 2 and subtract 1!

I don't get it ...

Sequences can be described using a formula where **n** is the term. By using a formula, you can figure out a number later in the sequence. In the sequence below, the formula would be 3n + 1.

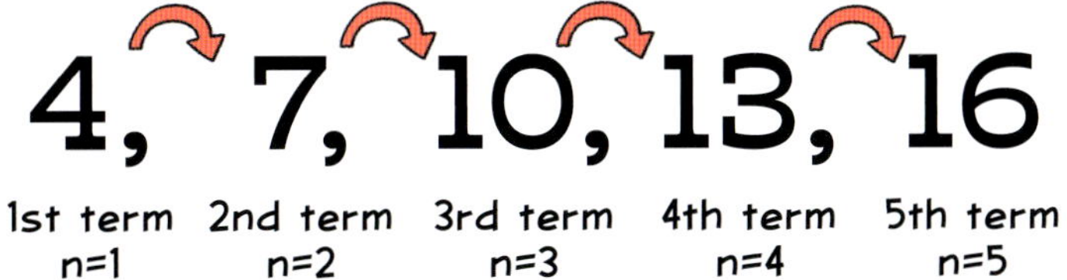

How to See a Sunflower

Beautiful! My **SUNFLOWER** has opened at last.

It's too tall! I can't see the top.

Come up here!

I didn't think you liked flowers, Professor.

I'm admiring the **MATHEMATICS**, Scooter ... the **FIBONACCI SEQUENCE!**

FIBO-WHAT?!

The **Fibonacci sequence** is a number sequence that begins with two 1s, then each number is the sum of the last two added together.

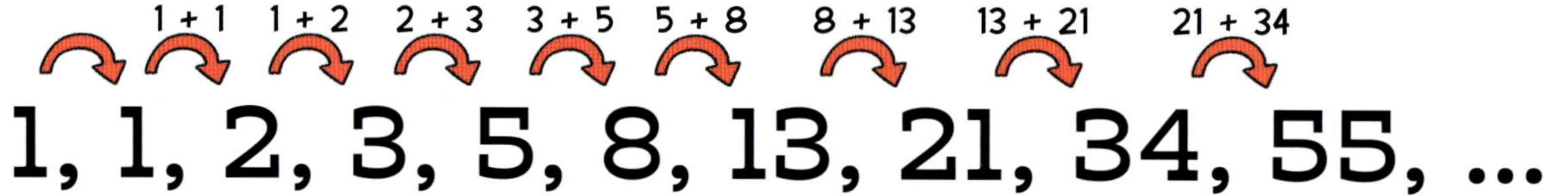

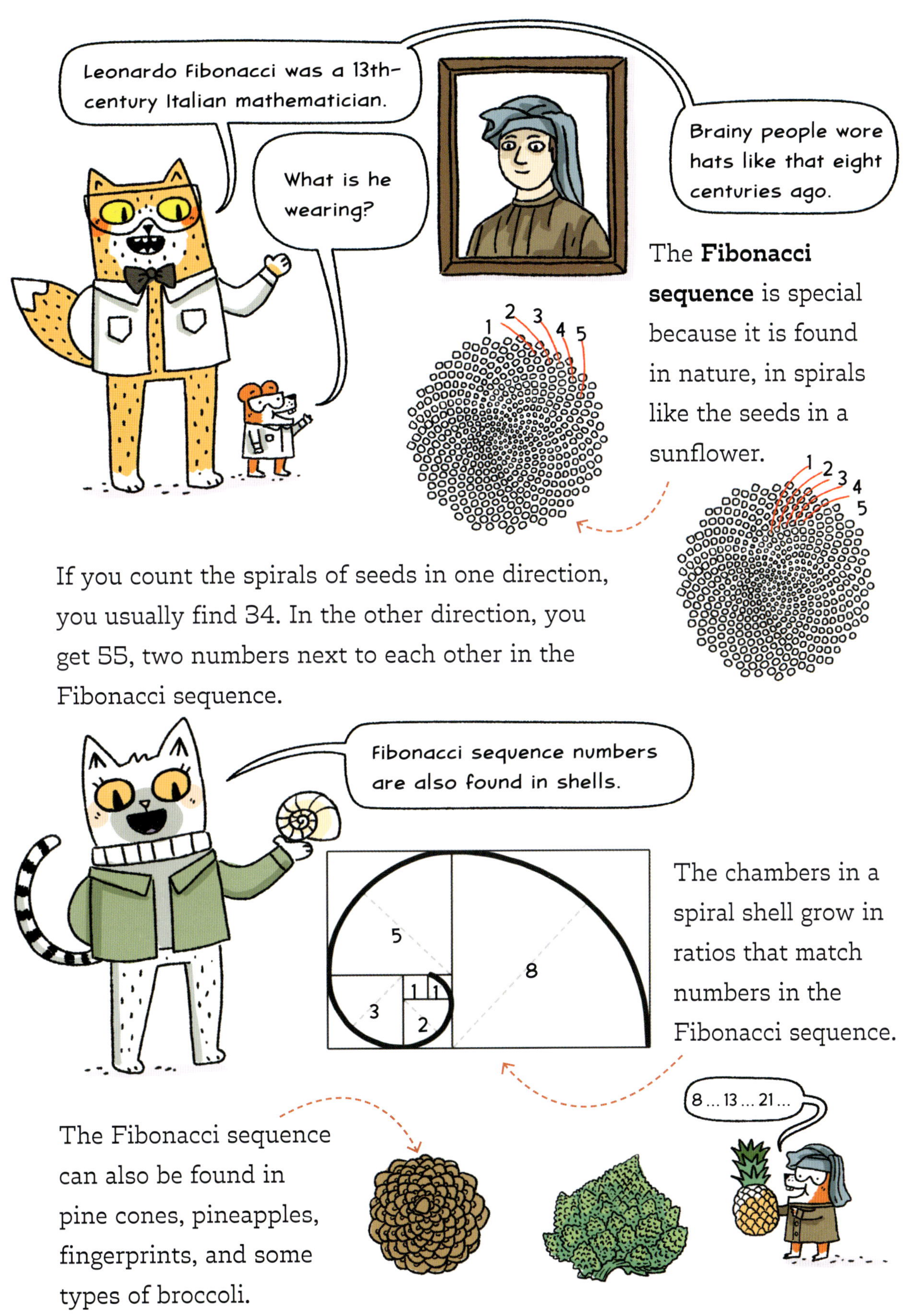

The **Fibonacci sequence** is special because it is found in nature, in spirals like the seeds in a sunflower.

If you count the spirals of seeds in one direction, you usually find 34. In the other direction, you get 55, two numbers next to each other in the Fibonacci sequence.

The chambers in a spiral shell grow in ratios that match numbers in the Fibonacci sequence.

The Fibonacci sequence can also be found in pine cones, pineapples, fingerprints, and some types of broccoli.

How to Do a Survey
Could you spare a few moments for my survey, Professor?
Go ahead.

What would you say are my best qualities, on a score from 1 to 10?
First, **HELPFULNESS**.

Hmm. I'll go with 5.
Only **5**?!
OK, 5-and-a-half.

How about **FRIENDLINESS**?
6. I mean, 7.

Eight questions later ...
Comparing to the scores I gave you, it seems I beat you in almost every category.

Let me see those results!

A survey collects information, or **data**, from a large group of people. This data can be organized into charts and graphs to make it easier to understand and compare results. The collection and organization of data is called **statistics**.

For example, you could do a survey of your friends' top foods ...

Once you have the figures, you can list them in a table, then arrange them in various ways.

Top food	Pizza	Cupcake	Burger	Chocolate	Noodle soup	Hot dog
Frequency	4	2	5	6	3	1

Charts have two axes—one vertical and one horizontal.

This **bar chart** makes it easy to see which are the least and most popular choices.

In this case, chocolate is the top food.

What's this, Scooter?

It's my candy bar chart.

Other ways of displaying data include line graphs and pie charts.

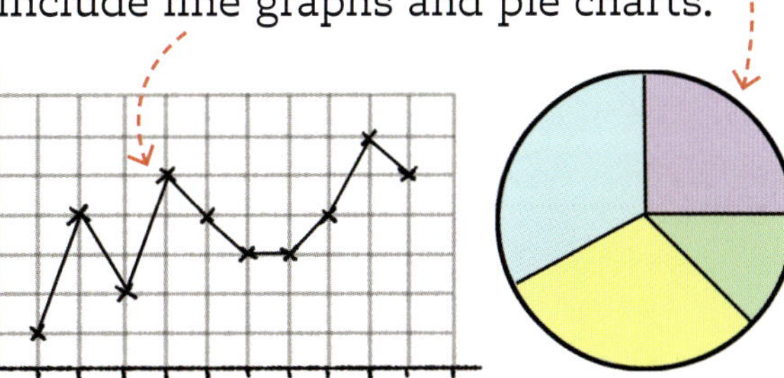

How to Be Top of the Charts
SIGH!
What's the matter, Professor?

I've made a chart to show how I spend each day.
30 minutes breakfast, 4 hours study, 1 hour lunch, 4 hours inventing, 1 hour exercise, 2 hours study, 2 hours dinner ...

... EIGHT HOURS SLEEPING!

I could be using that time for study and inventing gadgets ...
But we ALL need sleep! Even YOUR brain needs a rest.

Maybe I can sleep for just six hours a day ...
I have a BETTER idea. Instead of cutting your sleep ...

... use the time you waste WORRYING ABOUT IT!

Bar charts use bars of different heights to display data.

The simplest of bar charts compares different categories.

Bars can also be divided to show the choices of different groups of people for each category.

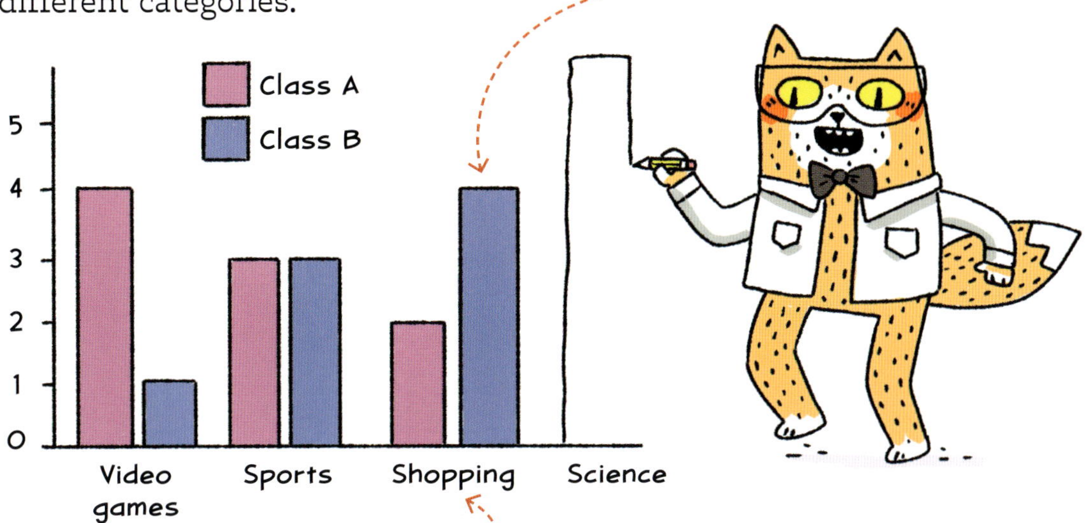

This bar chart shows the activities that Class A and Class B prefer.

A **compound bar chart** displays several types of information in each bar.

This chart shows the results for three soccer teams over 10 games.

Each color represents a win, a loss, or a draw.

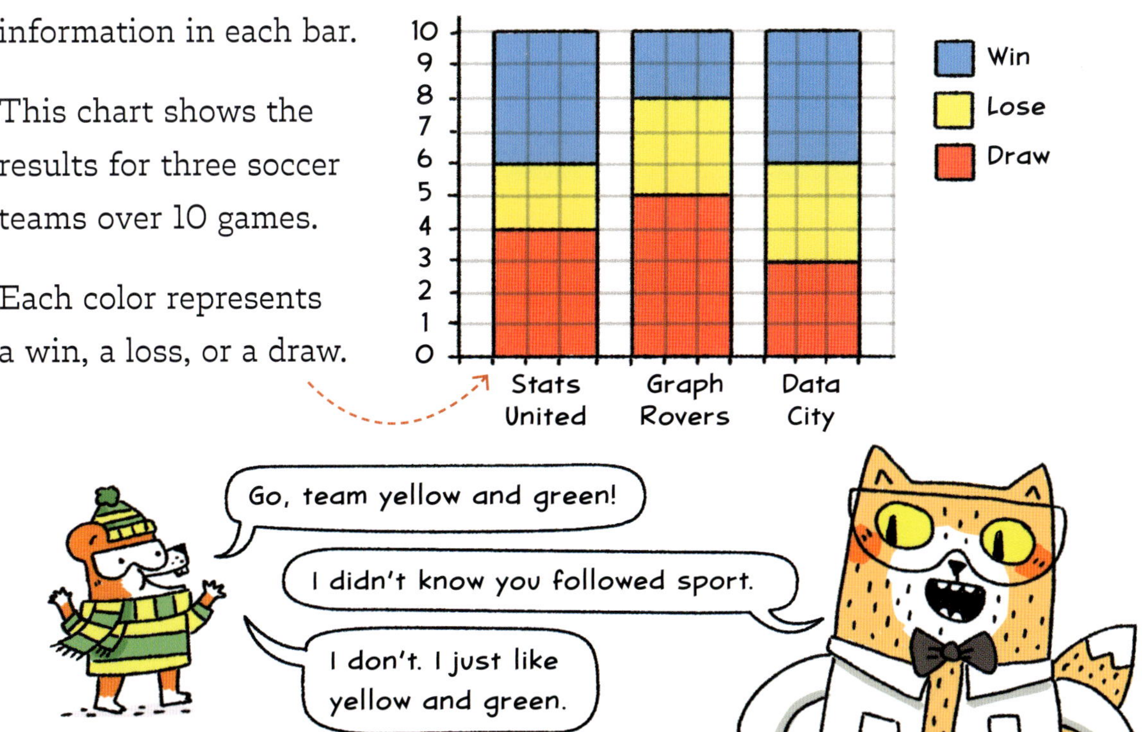

How to Divide a Pie
That's an impressive pie you baked, Scooter! What's inside it?

Well, I did a survey to find out everyone's top pie ingredients.

Here are the results.
The top choices were banana with maple syrup ...
... smoked fish ...

... apple and rhubarb ...
... and cheese and pumpkin.

But the most popular was chicken and mushroom.
So, which one did you choose?

ONE?!
I used ALL of them!

A **pie chart** is a way of displaying data by showing proportions of a whole.

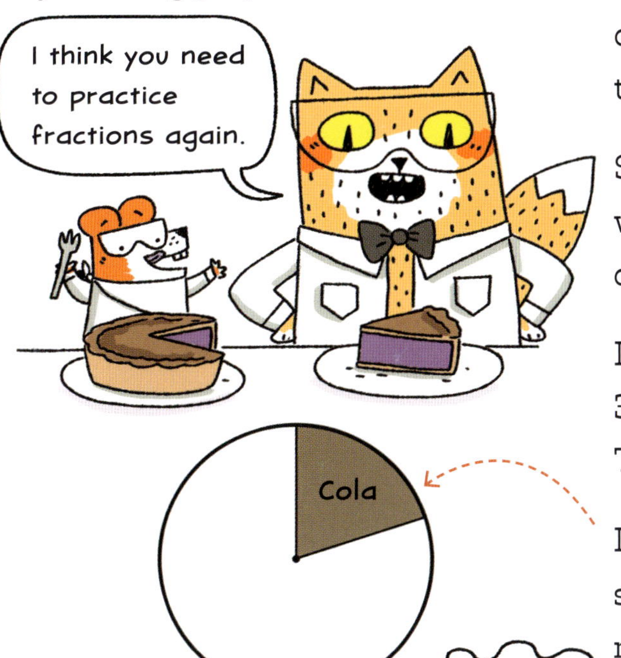

Like a round pie, the chart is divided into segments for each category. To draw a pie chart, you need to know the angle for each segment.

Since a circle has 360 degrees, you can work out the angle for one item by dividing 360 by the total frequency.

If 30 people took part in a survey, $360 \div 30 = 12$
Then multiply each answer by 12.

If 6 people chose cola, $6 \times 12 = 72$, so cola would have a segment measuring 72°.

Whoooooooa!

Here is a table showing the results, with 30 people each choosing their top sport.

Top sport	Soccer	Baseball	Bicycling	Tennis	Gymnastics
Frequency	8	6	4	5	7

To figure out the angle for each sport, multiply the numbers by 12.

Top sport	Soccer	Baseball	Bicycling	Tennis	Gymnastics
Angle	96°	72°	48°	60°	84°

Gymnastics
Tennis
Bicycling
Soccer
Baseball

Pie charts make it easy to compare results.

A big win for soccer!

How to Keep Track
I've been keeping records of my daily activity as you suggested.
What does this graph show?

This shows how many snacks I ate each day.

This shows how many hours of TV I watched, and this one shows how many naps I took.

This one adds up my bathroom breaks, and this shows how many times I sneezed.

And this one?

This shows how much graph paper I used.

A line graph is a good way of showing data collected over time.

The vertical axis on the graph shows the data recorded. The horizontal axis shows the time or date.

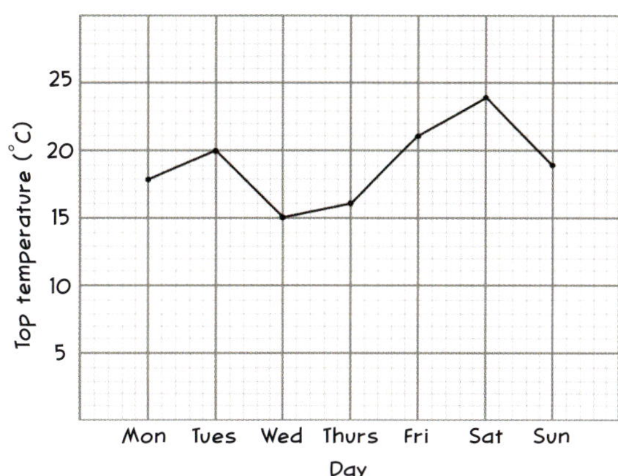

This graph shows the top temperature measured over seven days.
For each day a dot is placed to mark the temperature, following the scale on the left.

The dots are joined to show the pattern over the week as the temperature drops and rises.

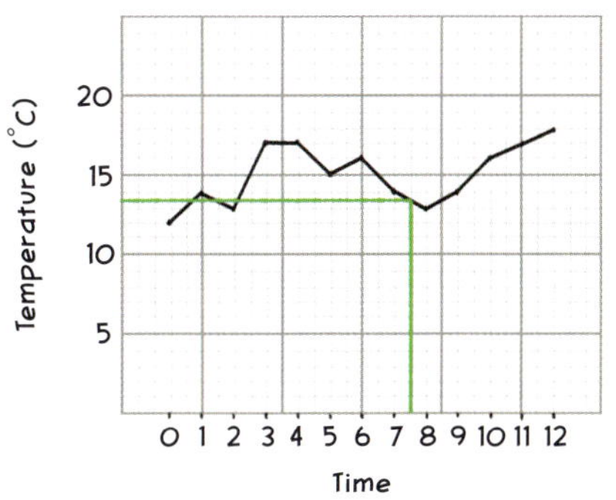

You can use a line graph to make estimates between measurements. The temperature at 7:30 am was about 13.5 °C (56 °F).

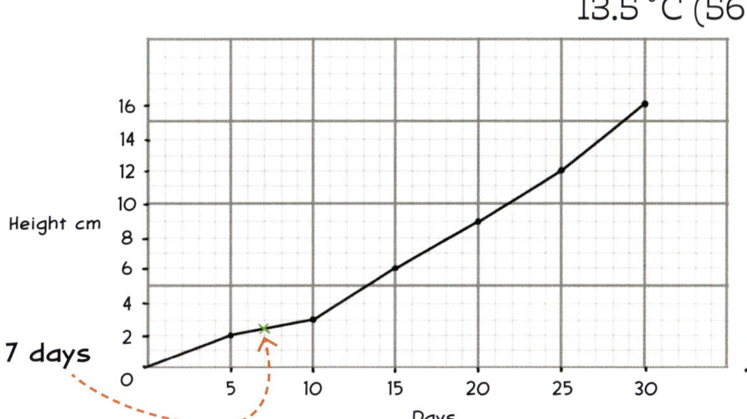

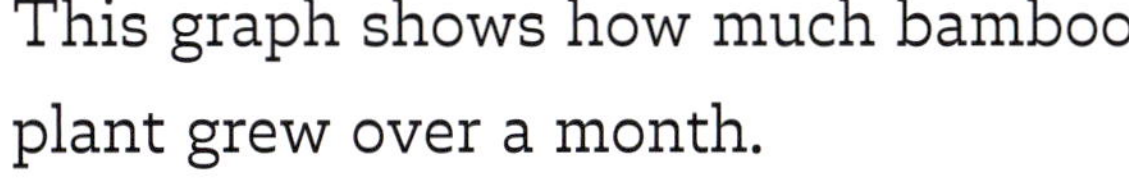

This graph shows how much bamboo plant grew over a month.

You can work out how much it grew in one week by checking the difference over 7 days.

How to Do Magic
Pick a card, any card.

Don't show it to me.
I will read your mind and get the answer.

GASP! Have you invented a MIND-READING GADGET?
No ... I'm going to use MAGIC!

I thought you didn't believe in ...
The card you chose was ...

The 5 OF DIAMONDS!
You're right! How did you do that?

I saw the reflection of your card on the computer screen!

These "magic tricks" are really mathematics, but they can surprise friends.

TRICK 1

Pick a number.

Add the next higher number to it.

Add 9 and divide by 2, and then subtract the original number.

TRICK 2

Pick a number between 1 and 10.

Add 2 to it.

Multiply by 2.

Subtract 2.

Divide by 2.

Subtract your original number.

TRICK 3

Pick a three-digit number with all three digits the same (such as 111, 222).

Add up the digits.

Divide the three-digit number by the last number.

How to Be Above Average
Would you say I'm **ABOVE AVERAGE** for a guinea pig?
I would need to know more guinea pigs to work out the average.

An hour later.
OK, I brought over some friends.
Hello, Professor!

Well, it seems you're **ABOVE AVERAGE** in height.

And **ABOVE AVERAGE** in weight.

Here's a knowledge test for you all to take.

Incredible! You got an **ABOVE AVERAGE** score, too!
You didn't just choose your shortest, lightest, and least smart friends, did you?
Um ...

An **average** is a middle value within a set of data. There are three types of average: the **mean**, **median**, and **mode**.

The **mean** is the value most people understand as the average.

To figure out the mean, add all the values together, and divide by the number of values.

$$\textbf{Mean} = \frac{\textbf{total of values}}{\textbf{number of values}}$$

$2 + 3 + 4 + 4 + 5 + 6 + 7 + 7 + 7 + 8 = 53$

$53 \div 10 = 5.3$, so 5.3 is the mean of this group.

I spent 5 dollars this week, 6 last week, and 4 the week before.

Then your mean spend is 5 + 6 + 4, divided by 3. That's 5 dollars!

It took me 21 minutes to bicycle to the store today, 24 minutes last week, 30 minutes the week before.

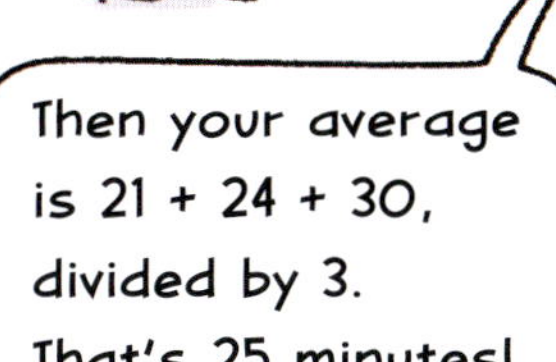

The **median** is the middle value when the figures are listed from smallest to largest.

For 2, 3, 4, 4, 5, 6, 7, 7, 7, 8, the middle is between 5 and 6, so the median is 5.5.

The **mode** is the value that appears most often.
In the list 2, 3, 4, 4, 5, 6, 7, 7, 7, 8, 7 is the mode.

Averages are useful for planning, to figure out how much money you might need for a month or how long a journey may take.

How to Avoid a Lightning Strike
I thought you said the weather forecast was **CLEAR**.
I was **CLEARLY** wrong.

BABOOM!
THUNDER! And where's there's thunder ...
We could get hit by **LIGHTNING**, Professor!

Calm down, Scooter. The probability of us being hit by lightning is close to **ZERO**.
PROBABILITY?

PROBABILITY is a measure of how likely something is to happen.
For example, if I flip a coin there is a 1 in 2 or $\frac{1}{2}$ chance of it landing on heads.

BOING!
Ow!

I don't want lightning to hit me on the head.

The chance of us **BOTH** being hit is even less.
KRACK ABOOM!

If there was a one in a million chance of one of us being hit, then the chance of us both being hit is one in a million **TIMES** a million, or one in a **TRILLION!**

If one of us gets hit, it's bound to be me.

There's even **LESS PROBABILITY** of you being hit by a meteorite.
Now I have to watch out for **METEORITES**, too!

WHOA!
SPLOOSH!

What was the **PROBABILITY** of you slipping into a **PUDDLE**?

How to Fold Paper More Than 7 Times
Why are you wearing your gym kit, Scooter?
I'm taking on a MAJOR PHYSICAL CHALLENGE!

Are you walking to the bakery?
Something even more challenging than that.

Are you running a MARATHON?
No, my legs are too short.

30 minutes with a HULA HOOP?
No, I get too dizzy.

50 PRESS UPS?
No ... something even harder!

I'm going to fold this piece of paper EIGHT TIMES!
GASP!

Trying to fold an average sheet of paper more than 7 times is almost impossible. This is because the paper soon gets too thick and small to fold.

If it were possible, after 27 folds an average sheet of (very large) paper would be thicker than the height of the world's tallest mountain!

The paper thickness doubles with each fold.
1st fold = 2 paper thicknesses
2nd fold = 4
3rd fold = 8 ...
7th fold = 128 ...
27th fold = 134,217,728 paper thicknesses,
13.4 km (8.3 miles) thick

Is it **REALLY** impossible to fold more than seven times?

If the paper is thin enough, it can be folded more than 7 times, but every fold makes the paper twice as thick and reduces it surface area by half. That's why a long, thin strip helps.

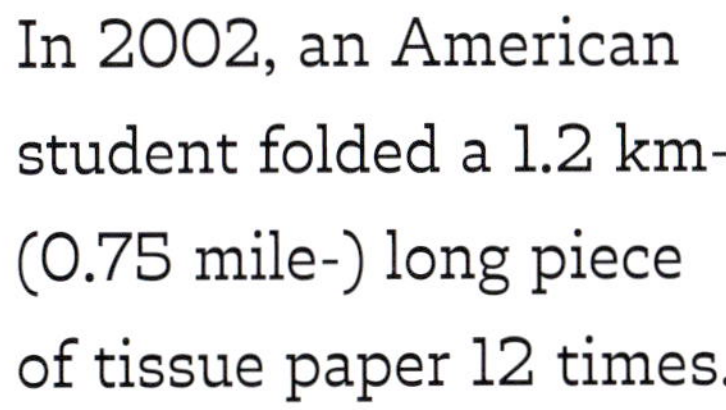

In 2002, an American student folded a 1.2 km- (0.75 mile-) long piece of tissue paper 12 times.

How to Keep a Secret
Spy Scooter taps in a secret number to open the locker and retrieve details of his new mission.

As usual, his instructions are in **CODE**.

Spy Scooter knows the code by heart.
4 7 12 19 – 4 19 ...

4 equals X, 7 equals I ...
That makes **XILW XW I DRQ FA BWI**.
Huh?!

I don't get it?
Didn't you read last week's message?

We updated the codes!

Mathematics can be used for codes.

The simplest codes involve replacing letters of the alphabet with numbers. A = 1, B = 2, C = 3, and so on.

To make it tricker to guess, you can start with a different number, A = 5, B = 6, or go backward.

You can also choose a word and base a code around it.

Like a **SCOOTER CODE?**

Exactly!

Choose a word that uses its different letters to start the number code: S = 1 C = 2 O = 3 T = 4 E = 5 R = 6.

Then replace the remaining letters of the alphabet, A=7, B=8, D=9, etc. All you need to do is share the code word to decode a message.

Or you can use an image as a clue to your code, such as a shape.

This pentagon has 5 sides. It could mean your code starts with A = 5.

This building has 8 windows. It could mean your code starts with A = 8.

Your code can have more than one step, too.

Did you just speak in code, because I didn't understand a word of it!

How to Speak to Aliens
BOOP - BEBE - BOO - BRRR!
What's that AWFUL noise?
It's a message for ALIENS.

Is it in an ALIEN language?
No, binary code.
BOOP - BEBE - BOO - BRRR!

The only language we might share with aliens is MATHEMATICS.
If they can translate the code, they will see pictures with a map to find Earth.

This message was sent into outer space over 50 years ago.
Have we heard anything back?
Not so far.

Greetings!
WAUGH!

Hi guys.
Are you OK?

On November 16, 1974, a radio message in binary code was sent from Earth toward a dense group of stars called M13, 25,000 light years away.

The message was sent in **binary code** since any aliens that might hear it would not be able to speak an Earth language, but they might understand basic mathematics.

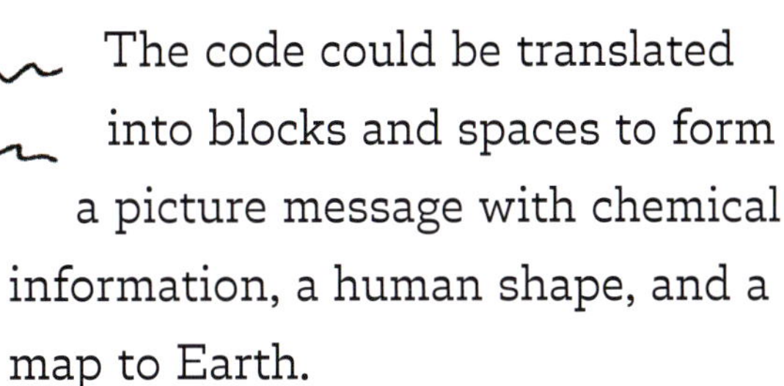

The code could be translated into blocks and spaces to form a picture message with chemical information, a human shape, and a map to Earth.

Why haven't we heard back? Are there no aliens?

At light speed, it would take 25,000 years for the message to reach its destination and another 25,000 years for us to hear a reply.

Mathematics is the language of the Universe. It explains how planets spin, stars burn, and galaxies evolve. It helps scientists plan the journeys for rockets and space probes.

And it may also turn out to be a way of saying hello to extraterrestrials!

010010 0110 11 010.

1101 100010 11.

Index